Betty Crocker's Diabetes COOKBOOK

Everyday Meals **EASY AS 1-2-3**

Wiley Publishing, Inc.

Library of Congress Cataloging-in-Publication Data:
Crocker, Betty.
    Betty Crocker's diabetes cookbook:
    everyday meals, easy as 1-2-3.
        p. cm.
Includes index.
    ISBN 0-7645-6704-7 (hardcover : alk. paper)
    1. Diabetes—Diet therapy—Recipes. I. Title:
    Diabetes cookbook. II.
    Title.
    RC662 .C755 2003
    641.5'6314—dc21
2002011322

Manufactured in China

10 9 8 7 6 5

General Mills, Inc.

Director, Books And Electronic Publishing: Kim Walter

Manager, Books: Lois L. Tlusty

Editor: Cheri A. Olerud

Recipe Development And Testing: Betty Crocker Kitchens

Food Styling: Betty Crocker Kitchens

Photography: General Mills Photo Studios and Image Center

International Diabetes Center

Richard M. Bergenstal, M.D., Endocrinologist, Executive Director, International Diabetes Center, Park Nicollet Clinic, Minneapolis

Diane Reader, R.D., L.D., C.D.E., Manager, Professional Education, International Diabetes Center, Park Nicollet Clinic, Minneapolis

Maureen Doran, R.D., L.D., Consultant, Registered Dietitian, Bell Institute of Health and Nutrition

A special thank you and acknowledgement to individuals with diabetes or their care-givers who were willing to advise and inspire others with the wisdom they gained as they learned to live with diabetes: Betty H., Bill A., Kate D., Lori S., Lynn H., Mary E., Michele H., Michelle M., Pat A., Sammy E., Sherry L., Steve T., Susan A., Tim H.

Wiley Publishing, Inc.

Publisher: Natalie Chapman

Executive Editor: Anne Ficklen

Editor: Caroline Schleifer

Production Editor: Heather Wilcox

Cover and Book Design: Edwin Kuo

Interior Layout: Holly Wittenberg

Manufacturing Buyer: Kevin Watt

Photography Art Director: Janet Skalicky

Cover photos: Baked Chicken and Rice with Autumn Vegetables (page 88); Italian Shrimp Stir-Fry (page 102); Creamy Vanilla-Caramel Cheesecake (page 232).

For more great ideas visit **www.bettycrocker.com**

Diabetes changes your life.

It requires daily planning, self-care, and a dose of determination. The good news is that living well with diabetes *is possible.* To make it easier, Betty Crocker has teamed up with the International Diabetes Center to bring you this unique cookbook. *Betty Crocker's Diabetes Cookbook* offers easy, delicious recipes the whole family will enjoy *and* provides the latest medical and nutritional information essential for people with diabetes.

Sound nutrition and good eating are at the heart of both diabetes care and prevention. Years of study show that the best food plan for someone with diabetes is no different than a healthy food plan for everyone. Making good food choices is the key! That's what makes *Betty Crocker's Diabetes Cookbook* so helpful. It can help anyone looking to eat healthy foods without sacrificing the satisfaction that comes with enjoying a good meal. The nutrition advice and recipes not only help a person manage diabetes better but can also, along with a physically active lifestyle, help *prevent* the development of diabetes.

Your diabetes food plan is designed to fit your lifestyle. It helps you select foods and recipes that will keep your blood glucose (sugar) levels as close to normal as possible, while keeping your weight in check. To help you do that, *Betty Crocker's Diabetes Cookbook* includes **Carbohydrate Choices** for every recipe. You'll also find invaluable medical, nutritional and food tips throughout. They include ideas for planning your next meal with family or friends, as well as reminders about the importance of blood pressure, cholesterol, eye exams, blood glucose testing, and more.

So enjoy the tastes, textures and aromas of all the wonderful recipes in *Betty Crocker's Diabetes Cookbook.* Eating well, doing moderate physical activity and having a positive outlook are the most important first steps toward living well with diabetes.

What's New with Carbohydrate Choices?

"Counting" carbohydrates with **Carbohydrate Choices** helps you track the amount of carbohydrate in a meal and balance that with your medication and activity. And that means you don't have to give up foods you like or that taste great. Can you ever have a piece of cake again? Yes! Once you know how to count carbohydrates, you'll be able to fit a wide variety of foods into your food plan, including sweets.

RICHARD M. BERGENSTAL, M.D.   DIANE READER, R.D.   MAUREEN DORAN, R.D.

Table of Contents

Living Well with Diabetes

The best-kept secret about diabetes food planning is that it is good for virtually everyone. You may think that people with diabetes need special foods prepared special ways, but as you look through this book, you may be surprised to see the wide variety of delicious and satisfying foods that you *can* eat. The key is moderation.

Carbohydrate Choices

If you have diabetes, you've come to the right place—this cookbook offers the **latest and easiest way to count Carbohydrate Choices.** These guidelines are easier than the exchange system because **you only need to keep track of one thing: the amount of carbohydrate that you eat for each meal and snack.** If you're used to keeping track of food exchanges, that information is included for you, too.

To create this cookbook, we've enlisted the experienced help of an endocrinologist (a diabetes specialist doctor) and two diabetes dietitians who have many years of experience working with people with diabetes. Teamed with the trusted recipes of the Betty Crocker Kitchens, you're sure to use and refer to this cookbook again and again.

Also included is valuable advice from others living with diabetes; they share the helpful tips that worked for them and the wisdom they gleaned as they learned to navigate the daily journey of what and how much to cook and eat.

The recipes in this cookbook were developed for healthy eating with diabetes, and **each recipe lists the Carbohydrate Choices per serving,** removing the guesswork for you. Use the seven sample menus and their Carbohydrate Choices (pages 238–241) as your guideline to planning complete meals for a full week. Keeping overall health and all-family appeal in mind, we've kept the fat, sugar and calories down, added whole grains, boosted the fiber and used a variety of spices and herbs to keep the lid on sodium—all without sacrificing the naturally delicious satisfying flavor of the food.

A diagnosis of diabetes may make you feel like your life is spinning out of control. One positive way to approach this news is to think of having diabetes as an opportunity to take charge of your health and find great pleasure in the foods you select and eat. Whether you've been recently diagnosed with diabetes, have been living with it for a while or are giving care to someone with diabetes, this book is your helpful tool on the road to better health.

Along with having great food options, it's important to know as much as you can about diabetes, how to take good care of yourself and how your diabetes care team can help you. This cookbook is packed with information that will guide you in taking the best possible care of your diabetes. The basics of good nutrition, a detailed explanation of how to use carbohydrate counting for food planning and a section on medical information for diabetes follows. Read it now, or use it as a refresher later. It's all right at your fingertips!

Who's at Greater Risk?

As the incidence of diabetes grows, more is understood about the disease and who is at risk. Regular testing is recommended for anyone who:

- Has a **family member with diabetes**, especially type 2 diabetes
- Is of **African American, Hispanic American, Native American, Southeast Asian or Pacific Islander** heritage
- Has had **gestational diabetes** or a baby weighing more than nine pounds at birth
- Leads a **sedentary or inactive** lifestyle
- Has components of the **"metabolic syndrome,"** which includes abnormal blood lipids (high triglycerides and low HDL—or "good"—cholesterol), high blood pressure, obesity, insulin resistance and polycystic ovary syndrome in women.

What Is Diabetes?

To understand diabetes, it's important to understand glucose and insulin. Glucose, a form of sugar, is the main fuel the body needs and uses for energy. It is made when the food you eat is broken down during digestion. Glucose travels through the bloodstream and enters the cells in the body with the help of insulin. Insulin, a hormone made in the pancreas, is the "key" that "opens" cells so glucose can get inside to provide the body with energy.

Diabetes develops when insulin is either completely absent, in short supply or poorly used by the body. Without insulin, too much glucose stays in the bloodstream rather than entering the cells to be used for energy. If diabetes is not diagnosed and treated, blood glucose levels continue to rise, and over time, can lead to serious health problems—the "complications" of diabetes, such as blindness, heart and blood vessel disease, stroke, kidney failure, nerve damage and limb amputation.

Taking care of your diabetes by eating the right foods, exercising regularly and taking your medication, if prescribed, helps you feel great and provides the best defense against complications.

Diabetes in the United States

More than 17 million Americans have diabetes. That's more than 6 percent of the U.S. population. One-third of Americans who have diabetes aren't even aware that they have it, and another 16 million Americans have "pre-diabetes." Pre-diabetes is a condition in which blood glucose is higher than normal but not yet high enough to be diabetes. In most cases, pre-diabetes will eventually progress into diabetes unless some action is taken. For those who are overweight, the most effective action appears to be losing weight and exercising regularly. There are also certain medications that may help to prevent the development of diabetes. Your healthcare provider can discuss your options with you. (For more on diabetes prevention, see page 37.)

The Types of Diabetes

There are three main types of diabetes:

Type 1

This type occurs most often in children and young adults under the age of thirty. Type 1 is an autoimmune disease in which the body's own immune system destroys the beta cells in the pancreas that produce insulin. The diagnosis of type 1 diabetes is usually signaled by common symptoms such as extreme thirst, significant weight loss and frequent urination. People with type 1 diabetes need to take daily insulin injections to stay alive.

Type 2

About 90 percent of people with diabetes have type 2 diabetes. It usually develops in adults over age forty, but a growing number of cases in younger people, including teens and children, are diagnosed each year. With type 2 diabetes, the cells in the body "resist" the action of insulin, and glucose doesn't get into the cells very well. This is called insulin resistance. Over time, the insulin-producing cells in the pancreas wear out, in part because they're working too hard trying to overcome the body's insulin resistance.

Gestational

Gestational diabetes occurs when the hormonal changes of pregnancy demand more insulin than the body can make or use well. Three to five percent of pregnant women develop it, usually during the second or third trimester (twenty-four to twenty-eight weeks). Though gestational diabetes usually disappears after the baby is born, its occurrence significantly increases the risk for developing type 2 diabetes later in life.

Diabetes is indeed epidemic. Why? In large part, diabetes has spread because high-fat-and-calorie diets and lack of exercise have lead to obesity, a major risk factor for diabetes. A similar trend is occurring in other countries as well. As people in other countries become more affluent, consume more food and are less active, the rate of diabetes is increasing rapidly. It's estimated that there will be 300 million people with diabetes worldwide by the year 2025.

Eating Well for Good Health

Most people agree that eating is one of the greatest joys in life, and that does not have to change just because you have diabetes. Food plays a key role in many family celebrations and social and work situations. Viewing diabetes as an opportunity to prepare and eat the best possible foods to maintain your body will help you deal with the daily challenge of diabetes.

At first, it may be a struggle when others are planning a "normal" holiday dinner, for example; but with experience, you'll be able to modify recipes or situations to fit your needs. And it's likely that eventually you'll like your new way of eating much better than the old way. An added benefit is you will feel better, both physically and emotionally. The whole family can also reap the rewards of eating well. Who knows, someday they may even thank you for showing them how to begin healthy eating habits!

The Role of Carbohydrate Foods

Food contains three main nutrients: **carbohydrate**, **protein** and **fat**. It's the carbohydrate foods that raise your blood glucose level, so you need to pay attention to how much you eat. Foods that contain carbohydrate include starches, fruit, milk, some milk products and sweets.

Carbohydrate foods are necessary for good nutrition. They provide important nutrients,

Blood Tests: Doctor's Tool to Diagnose

If you have two or more risk factors, you should be tested for diabetes as part of your regular checkup. Three different blood tests may be used to diagnose diabetes:

Fasting blood glucose test
Blood is drawn after at least eight hours of not eating or drinking anything (usually first thing in the morning).

Casual blood glucose test
Blood may be drawn at any time.

Glucose tolerance test
Blood for this test is drawn two hours after drinking a special glucose solution. The chart below shows blood glucose ranges for pre-diabetes, diabetes and no diabetes (normal).

Blood Test Table

Diagnosis	Fasting Test	Casual Test or Glucose Tolerance Test
Pre-diabetes	110–125 mg/dL	140–199 mg/dL
Diabetes	126 mg/dL or higher	200 mg/dL or higher
Normal	less than 110 mg/dL	less than 140mg/dL

Used with permission from International Diabetes Center, Minneapolis, MN

vitamins and minerals, and they give your body the energy it needs. Without carbohydrates, your body cannot function properly, although, as with any foods, it's wise to eat carbohydrates in moderation to avoid excess calories and weight gain. Carbohydrate foods include starches such as grains and grain-based foods such as rice, bread, cereal, pasta, and starchy vegetables such as corn, squash and potatoes. Milk and yogurt, fruits and fruit juices and sweets are also carbohydrate foods. All carbohydrates provide four calories per gram of carbohydrate. Eating consistent amounts of carbohydrate according to your diabetes food plan will help control your blood glucose levels.

Diabetes Nutrition 101

The primary goal in diabetes care is blood glucose control, followed closely by the need to control blood fats and blood pressure, and to minimize weight gain, all of which play a significant role in diabetes health.

At the foundation of achieving all of these goals is good nutrition. A nutritious, well-balanced diet provides the building blocks for healthy body functioning, physical energy, satisfaction in eating and just feeling good!

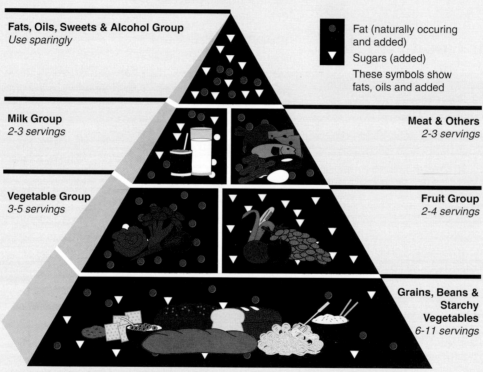

Fats, Oils, Sweets & Alcohol Group
Use sparingly

● Fat (naturally occuring and added)
▼ Sugars (added)
These symbols show fats, oils and added

Milk Group
2-3 servings

Meat & Others
2-3 servings

Vegetable Group
3-5 servings

Fruit Group
2-4 servings

Grains, Beans & Starchy Vegetables
6-11 servings

Reprinted with permission from The American Diabetes Association

Using the Food Pyramid

The Diabetes Food Guide Pyramid divides food into six groups based on similar nutrition content. The five lower parts represent the five different food groups that make up most of your diet. The top of the pyramid, labeled "Fats, Oils, Sweets and Alcohol," shows foods that should be limited, but don't need to be eliminated. The numbers next to each food group tell you how many servings are recommended from that particular group for each day.

Your body needs foods from all of the food groups. Your dietitian will help you develop a *personal food plan* that tells the specific number of servings from each group that you need to eat each day for good nutrition. Eating consistent amounts of foods at consistent times is a key factor in your blood glucose control. Counting Carbohydrate Choices makes it easier to eat consistently from day to day.

Carbohydrate Counting

Carbohydrate is measured in grams. A gram is a small unit of weight in the metric system. The trick to carbohydrate counting is to know how many carbohydrate grams you are eating at any given time. Carbohydrate counting provides you with a tool to help with blood glucose control and enables you to select the amount of carbohydrate recommended by your healthcare provider for a well-balanced diet. Research is underway to further define the proper mix of protein, fat and carbohydrate to help a person maintain optimal health.

A typical diabetes food plan includes 3 to 5 Carbohydrate Choices (see *What Is a Carbohydrate Choice?* on page 13) for meals, depending upon your gender and food planning goals. Snacks are usually 1 to 2 Choices, if they are included in your plan. You and your dietitian will determine how much carbohydrate you should eat each day. Then together, you will find the best way to space carbohydrate foods throughout the day so that you get the energy you need without overwhelming your body's insulin supply. Or, if you take insulin, your diabetes care provider will help determine the right doses to match the amount of carbohydrate food you eat. Every meal and snack needs to include carbohydrate foods, because that is what your body "runs" on.

It's best to follow your food plan. "Saving" Carbohydrate Choices from one meal or snack to have at another time can lead to low or high blood glucose levels. If you want to eat more than your food plan calls for, you'll need to make up for it with extra exercise or additional insulin.

Your dietitian can tell you more about eating "outside" your food plan. But be careful—eating more of any food adds calories and potentially weight, whether you have diabetes or not.

Carbohydrate on Food Labels

While there are many "standard" 1-Carbohydrate-Choice foods, such as milk, fruit and bread, you may also want to eat carbohydrate-containing foods such as pizza, frozen dinners or frozen yogurt. How do these foods translate into Carbohydrate Choices? Look to the nutrition label on the food package.

Nutrition labels on packaged foods provide the carbohydrate content of that specific product. Finding the carbohydrate on a Nutrition Facts panel of a food package is easy. Begin by looking at the serving size of the food. Looking down the panel, locate the carbohydrate grams for that serving. "Total Carbohydrate" includes all starches, sugars and dietary fiber.

You can use the *How Many Carbohydrate Choices?* conversion guide (page 12) to convert the number of carbohydrate grams on any label to the number of Carbohydrate Choices.

FIBER ONE® Bran Cereal

Nutrition Facts

Serving Size ½ cup (30g)
Servings Per Container About 15

Amount Per Serving	Fiber One	with ½ cup skim milk
Calories	60	100
Calories from Fat	10	10

	% Daily Value**	
Total Fat 1g*	**1%**	**2%**
Saturated Fat 0g	**0%**	**0%**
Polyunsaturated Fat 0g		
Monounsaturated Fat 0g		
Cholesterol 0mg	**0%**	**1%**
Sodium 130mg	**5%**	**8%**
Potassium 240mg	**7%**	**13%**
Total Carbohydrate 24g	**8%**	**10%**
Dietary Fiber 14g	**57%**	**57%**
Soluble Fiber 1g		
Sugars 0g		
Other Carbohydrate 10g		
Protein 2g		

Vitamin A	0%	4%
Vitamin C	10%	10%
Calcium	10%	25%
Iron	25%	25%
Vitamin D	0%	10%
Thiamin	25%	30%
Riboflavin	25%	35%
Niacin	25%	25%
Vitamin B₆	25%	25%
Folic Acid	25%	25%
Vitamin B₁₂	25%	35%
Phosphorus	15%	30%
Magnesium	15%	20%
Zinc	25%	30%
Copper	8%	8%

*Amount in Cereal. A serving of cereal plus skim milk provides 1g total fat, less than 5mg cholesterol, 190mg sodium, 440mg potassium, 30g total carbohydrate (6g sugars) and 6g protein.
**Percent Daily Values are based on a 2,000 calorie diet. Your daily values may be higher or lower depending on your calorie needs:

	Calories:	2,000	2,500
Total Fat	Less than	65g	80g
Sat Fat	Less than	20g	25g
Cholesterol	Less than	300mg	300mg
Sodium	Less than	2,400mg	2,400mg
Potassium		3,500mg	3,500mg
Total Carbohydrate		300g	375g
Dietary Fiber		25g	30g

How Many Carbohydrate Choices?

Use this conversion guide to convert the number of carbohydrate grams to Carbohydrate Choices. If a food has 5 or more grams of fiber, subtract the total grams of fiber from the total carbohydrate before determining the Carbohydrate Choices. (See **Fiber,** page 14, for more information.)

Carbohydrate Choices	Total Carbohydrate Grams (g)
0	0–5
1/2	6–10
1	11–20
1 1/2	21–25
2	26–35
2 1/2	36–40
3	41–50
3 1/2	51–55
4	56–65
4 1/2	66–70
5	71–80

Used with permission from International Diabetes Center, Minneapolis, MN

What About Sugar?

Sugar is a carbohydrate. It affects your blood glucose in the same way that other carbohydrates do. Contrary to what many believe, people with diabetes can eat some sweets and foods with added sugar as long as the carbohydrate is counted.

Desserts and tempting sweets can pack a big carbohydrate wallop—even small portions. If you decide to eat a food with added sugar, you need to plan by substituting it for other carbohydrates in your food plan. For example, a two-inch-square piece of cake with frosting has the same amount of carbohydrate as one cup of corn or two slices of bread, but it also contains more fat and calories than the corn or the bread.

Often, foods high in added sugar have little or no nutritional value other than calories. And usually, where there is sugar, there is also fat, so it makes good sense to monitor the sweets you eat.

About Exchange Lists

If you've had diabetes for a while, you may have learned to use the Exchange Lists. If so, you already know a lot about food groups and counting. What's the advantage of Carbohydrate Choices over diet (food) exchanges? Carbohydrate counting is an easier way to manage the food you eat and offers you more flexibility in food selection, making meal planning easier. If you'd like to make the switch to counting Carbohydrate Choices, you'll probably find it much easier than the exchange system.

Carbohydrate Counting Tips

- A good start is to remember that 15 grams of carbohydrate is 1 Choice.
- One starch, fruit or milk exchange is equal to 1 Carbohydrate Choice. All the foods in these three groups raise blood glucose the same.
- Meats and fats aren't counted because they do not contain carbohydrate.
- Nonstarchy vegetables (any vegetable except corn, peas, squash and potatoes) are not counted unless eaten in large (3 cups raw or 1 1/2 cups cooked) quantities.
- If a food has 5 or more grams of fiber, subtract the total grams of fiber from the total carbohydrate before determining the Carbohydrate Choices.

Essential Nutrients for Good Health

In addition to carbohydrate, there are several nutrients needed every day to maintain optimal health. It's important to balance your intake of proteins and fat as well as carbohydrates as part of a healthy diet. Just as eating too much carbohydrate may lead to excess calories and weight, a diet that's too high in protein and fat but low in carbohydrate won't provide your body with the energy and balanced nutrition it needs for proper functioning. The bottom line is moderation. Low-fat meat and dairy products (with an emphasis on increasing mononsaturated fats) along with a moderate amount of nutritious carbohydrate foods that fit your food plan are the keys to healthy, satisfying eating.

Protein is found in meats, poultry, fish, milk and other dairy products, eggs, dried peas and beans and nuts. Starch and vegetables also have small amounts of protein. Your body uses protein for growth and maintenance. Protein provides four calories per gram. Most Americans eat more protein than their bodies need. Your dietitian will help you determine how much protein is right for your body. Five to seven ounces of protein foods per day are typically recommended. Choosing low-fat meats and dairy products also offers heart-healthy benefits to people with diabetes.

Fat is found in butter, margarine, oils, salad dressings, nuts, seeds, cheese, meat, fish, poultry, snack foods, ice cream, cookies and many desserts. Your body needs some fat for good nutrition, just as it needs protein and carbohydrate. But certain types of fat are better for you than others. There are three different types of fat: monounsaturated, polyunsaturated and saturated. Unsaturated fats are sometimes hydrogenated (hydrogen is added to them) to help make them solid at room temperature. This process creates trans fatty acids. Health

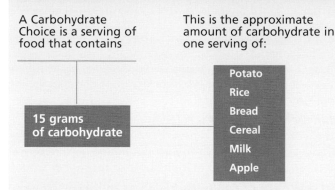

What Is a Carbohydrate Choice?

A Carbohydrate Choice is a serving of food that contains

15 grams of carbohydrate

This is the approximate amount of carbohydrate in one serving of:

Potato
Rice
Bread
Cereal
Milk
Apple

If you eat two apples, it counts as 2 Carbohydrate Choices. If you eat one slice of bread and one cup of milk that also counts as 2 Carbohydrate Choices. Your customized food plan will include the right number of Carbohydrate Choices for you. (See pages 244–245 for Carbohydrate Choices of Common Foods.)

professionals recommend eating less saturated and trans fats. These are found in meats; dairy products; coconut, palm and palm kernel oils; partially hydrogenated oils and fats that are hard at room temperature such as butter, shortening and margarine. Saturated fats and trans fats have been proven to raise blood cholesterol levels and can contribute to heart disease. The best choice is monounsaturated fat, which has been shown to improve the cardiovascular system. Monounsaturated fat is found in canola oil, olive oil, nuts and avocados. Polyunsaturated fat, found in corn oil, soybean oil and sunflower oil, is also a better choice than saturated fat.

Fat provides nine calories per gram. This is more than twice the calories found in carbohydrate or protein. Excess calories from fat are very easily stored in the body as fat and can lead to weight gain. It's not healthy to completely cut fats from your diet, especially monounsaturated fats. But most people can afford to reduce the amount of

Make Wise Food Choices a Habit

These tips are based on sound nutrition principles and are good for everyone—with or without diabetes.

- *Don't Skip Meals.* For many reasons you may be tempted to skip meals. This isn't a good idea, particularly if you have diabetes. When you skip meals, maintaining stable blood glucose levels becomes difficult. To make matters worse, people usually end up overeating at the next meal. So stick to your food plan, and for those days when that's not possible, talk to your dietitian to find appropriate snack choices to hold you over until your next meal.

- *Plan Meals and Snacks.* Planning what to eat for meals and snacks may seem overwhelming at first, but in time, you'll become an expert on what foods work best for you. If you don't plan, you may find yourself eating whatever is available, which may not be the best foods for you. Before you go shopping, decide on healthy meals and snacks to eat at home or take to work or school for the upcoming week.

- *Eat a Variety of Foods.* Grains, fruits and vegetables are packed with vitamins, minerals and fiber. Foods differ in their nutrient content, so eat a variety of colors and kinds, and be sure to include protein in your daily diet. Variety helps to ensure that your body gets the nutrients it needs for good health. Variety also helps to avoid boredom, which often leads to poor control.

- *Choose Low-Fat Foods Often.* Whenever you have the choice, drink fat-free (skim) milk, eat low-fat cheeses, yogurt and puddings, and use low-fat ingredients for cooking and baking, such as yogurt and light sour cream. Also, choose lean meats and remove the skin from chicken. When buying processed foods, look for those that contain 3 grams of fat or less per 100 calories.

calories they get from fat. Two of the best steps you can take are to reduce your fat intake and to switch to a more beneficial type of fat.

Fiber is necessary to maintain a healthy digestive tract and to help lower blood cholesterol levels. Experts recommend at least 25 grams of fiber daily. To get enough fiber each day, include:

- **Bran cereals or whole-grain breads, cereals, rice, pasta and other whole-grain products**
- **Vegetables and fruits, especially those with edible skins, seeds and hulls**
- **Legumes (dried beans and peas) and nuts**

Foods high in fiber are a good choice. If a food has 5 or more grams of fiber, you can subtract the total grams of fiber from the total carbohydrate before determining the number of Carbohydrate Choices. For example, look at the Fiber One label (page 11). The total number of fiber grams in one serving is 14. Since that is more than 5 grams, you can subtract it from the total carbohydrate grams in one serving. That leaves you with 10 grams of carbohydrate per serving or 1/2 Carbohydrate Choice. It's that simple! Most foods do not contain more than 5 grams of fiber, so check the food label carefully. Your best bet for finding high-fiber packaged foods are cereals, foods with bran and beans.

Water is essential for good health. Experts generally recommend eight to ten glasses of water daily for healthy individuals who do not have trouble with eliminating fluids from the body. Drink even more when it's hot, you're exercising or you don't feel well.

Vitamins help release energy from the fuel sources of carbohydrate, protein and fat. Your vision, hair, skin and the strength of your bones all depend on the vitamins that come from the foods you eat. The more variety you have in your diet, the more likely you are to get all the vitamins your body needs.

Minerals help your body with many functions. Iron, for example, carries much-needed oxygen to your body cells. Calcium is key to strong bones and teeth, and potassium is important for proper nerve and muscle function. Magnesium is also very important for proper body functioning and is often deficient in people with diabetes. The best way to get enough of the minerals you need is through a varied diet, although people with certain health conditions, including people with diabetes, sometimes need a supplement. It's a good idea to check with your healthcare provider about your individual needs.

Nutrition in the Recipes

In addition to the number of Carbohydrate Choices, each recipe in this cookbook lists the calories, calories from fat, fat, saturated fat, cholesterol, sodium, carbohydrate, dietary fiber and protein per serving. Food exchanges are also listed on each recipe. Based on criteria set by the American Dietetic Association and the American Diabetes Association, exchanges are listed as whole or half. To calculate the nutrition content of recipes, these guidelines were followed:

- **The first ingredient is used whenever a choice is given (such as 1/3 cup plain yogurt or sour cream).**
- **The first ingredient amount is used whenever a range is given (such as 2 to 3 teaspoons).**
- **The first serving number is used whenever a range is given (such as 4 to 6 servings).**
- **"If desired" ingredients are not included in the nutrition calculations, whether mentioned in the ingredient list or in the recipe directions as a suggestion (such as "top with sour cream if desired").**
- **Only the amount of a marinade or frying oil that is absorbed during preparation is calculated.**

Ask the Dietitian

Diane Reader and Maureen Doran, registered dietitians each with over twenty-five years of experience in nutrition counseling, answer the most frequently asked questions from people with diabetes.

Q. I've heard about the glycemic index. What is it?

A. The *glycemic index* is a rating system that predicts how high blood glucose levels will rise after you eat a specific food containing carbohydrates. It uses a scale of numbers to show which foods cause the highest to the lowest rises in blood glucose.

Choosing carbohydrates that cause a lower rise in blood glucose may help control the surge in blood glucose that occurs after eating. Whole grains, beans, fruit and non-starchy vegetables are low-glycemic foods. To discover this for yourself, test your blood glucose before and two hours after eating. You will notice that some foods raise your blood glucose higher, even though they have the same amount of carbohydrate.

Not everyone agrees that using the glycemic index is the best way to plan your carbohydrate intake. Most carbohydrate foods aren't eaten alone. Once foods are mixed, the glycemic response in your body may change. Also, the glycemic index doesn't take the nutritional values of foods into account. If you would like more information about the potential benefit of the glycemic index, discuss it with your diabetes care team.

Q. How does losing weight help my diabetes?

A. Losing weight, even ten to twenty pounds, can help people with type 2 diabetes by lowering insulin resistance, allowing your body's insulin to do a better job of controlling blood glucose levels. Weight loss can also improve blood fat and blood pressure levels. If you have diabetes, you're two to five times more likely to get cardiovascular disease than most people, and lowering blood pressure and blood fats reduces that risk. Remember that losing weight, along with more exercise, also helps prevent the development of diabetes if you have pre-diabetes or other risk factors for diabetes.

Q. Will vitamins, minerals or herbs help my diabetes?

A. Your dietitian can determine your overall nutrition status by taking a complete diet history and reviewing specific lab values. If you have a vitamin or mineral deficiency, it could be causing problems with your glucose control. For example, research has shown that taking the trace mineral *chromium* improved glucose control in those who had a chromium deficiency. If you eat a variety of vegetables, grains, meats and fruits each day, you probably don't need to take vitamin supplements. Ask your care team if you have any concerns.

Some herbs are thought to have glucose-lowering effects, but not enough studies have been done on any herb to advise taking herbal supplements. Always check with your doctor or dietitian before trying any; some herbs may interact adversely with diabetes medication.

Q. I've heard about very low carbohydrate diets, like Protein Power and Atkins. Should I try one of these diets?

A. Low-carbohydrate diets—high in fat and protein and very low in carbohydrates—are trendy today. Although such diets have some scientific rationale (less carbohydrate means fewer calories, lower insulin needs and potentially greater weight loss) in practice the results to date have not been optimal. A person may lose weight, but it may be at the expense of heart or kidney health. Also, these diets don't help people adopt the lifelong healthy eating habits that are key to weight loss success, and they also lack many of the important nutrients found in fruits and grains. People who've tried these diets find that they are depriving themselves of many foods they enjoy. This sets them up for failure because deprivation is not an answer to weight management and usually any weight loss they experience is temporary. The cycle begins: deprivation, failure, guilt, then deprivation again.

Your current weight may not be the healthiest weight for you. The best approach is to sit down with your diabetes care team and identify a healthy weight goal. To begin, work with your dietitian to develop a food plan that is customized to your needs. Add physical activity to your routine to burn calories.

Q. In addition to watching my weight, what are some other things I can do?

A. In addition to keeping your blood glucose levels in target, there are several things you can do to reduce your risk for complications or to prevent them from progressing.

- **If you smoke, try to quit. This may be the single most important thing you can do to reduce your risk of vascular disease.**
- **Make daily physical activity part of your routine. Check with your provider, however, to see what kind of activity is safe if you have diabetes complications.**
- **Eat foods low in saturated fat and salt to help achieve and maintain healthy blood lipid and blood pressure levels.**
- **Check your feet every day for cuts, signs of infection and thick calluses, and address any problems promptly.**
- **Visit your diabetes care team two to four times a year.**

Diabetes Care

No matter what type of diabetes you have, the diagnosis can feel overwhelming. It may seem that there is so much to know and to do; and in the midst of it, you are trying to adjust to this new reality in your life. To live well with diabetes, you need to incorporate **self-care** and **medical care** into your life to achieve your **treatment goals**.

Diabetes Care: It's in Your Hands

To live well with diabetes, you need to take charge of your care. Your diabetes knowledge, self-care skills and emotional health are in the palm of your hand.

Your diabetes care team provides the medical care you need to achieve your treatment goals, keeping good health at your fingertips. It's all in your hands.

Used with permission from International Diabetes Center, Minneapolis, MN

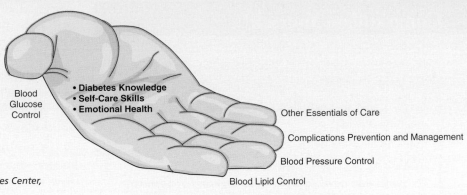

Blood Glucose Control

- **Diabetes Knowledge**
- **Self-Care Skills**
- **Emotional Health**

Other Essentials of Care

Complications Prevention and Management

Blood Pressure Control

Blood Lipid Control

Take Charge of Your Care

It takes a team to manage diabetes, and you are the central person on your team. Your diabetes care team may include your primary care provider, a nurse educator, a dietitian, an endocrinologist (diabetes specialist) and a mental health professional. Their expertise and guidance are invaluable, so seek them out whenever you need to.

Just remember, it's your body, and you know it better than anyone else. Listen to your body, and talk with your team about what you "hear." They can help you interpret and understand the signals you receive. Diabetes self-care is knowing what to do to take care of your diabetes and how to do it. Ongoing diabetes care and education will help ensure that you keep on track and stay healthy.

 ### 1. Diabetes Knowledge

Knowing about diabetes empowers you to take control of it, instead of allowing diabetes to take control of you. Understanding what is happening in your body and why it's happening can help you appreciate how you can make real differences in your health.

If you have not met with a diabetes educator or have not attended a diabetes education class, ask your health-care provider about education opportunities. If it's been a while since you've had diabetes education, check with your provider to see if there is a refresher course or an advanced class you can take. New information and approaches to diabetes treatment are emerging as scientists continue to study the disease. Ongoing diabetes education will ensure that you are informed of new advances as they become known.

 ### 2. Self-Care Skills

In diabetes education, you also learn the skills and lifestyle behaviors that contribute to controlling blood glucose levels day to day. These include **testing your blood glucose, following a**

Diabetes Treatment Goals

The overall goals of diabetes treatment are to:

- **Achieve and maintain blood glucose control**
- **Achieve and maintain optimal blood lipid (fat) levels**
- **Achieve and maintain healthy blood pressure levels**
- **Prevent or effectively treat diabetes complications**
- **Improve overall health**

Congratulate Yourself!

You're the best person to decide what accomplishments to celebrate, how to celebrate, when and with whom. Here are a few ideas to get you going:

- Go for a walk in a new nature area, cross-country ski or meditate outside.

- Catch up on some much-needed rest, or start reading a good book.

- Try something new: yoga, ballroom dancing or a gardening class in your community.

food plan and incorporating physical activity. Many people bring a family member, friend, spouse or significant other to education visits, which is a great way to include them and to get support for your diabetes self-care. Having someone in your life who understands diabetes can be very helpful and comforting.

Blood Glucose Testing. Regularly testing your blood glucose with a blood glucose meter, and keeping a record of your test results, helps you and your health-care provider assess how well your treatment plan is working. Testing also helps you:

- Evaluate your blood glucose control

- Decide what treatment or lifestyle changes to make to improve your control

- See how treatment or lifestyle changes affect your blood glucose levels

Your health-care provider can help you select a blood glucose meter that fits your needs. Diabetes technology is constantly advancing; several meters are available with a variety of different features and capabilities. Some even allow you to test just a small pinpoint of blood on your arm instead of your finger, and some give a reading in just seconds. There are also new devices that allow you to get a blood sample with very little discomfort.

Blood glucose targets for people with diabetes are a little higher than the normal range. Although we have excellent treatments for diabetes, they are not yet perfect, and many things in daily life affect blood glucose levels. So your blood glucose test results may sometimes be outside your target range—that's okay. Your blood glucose levels don't have to be perfect. The goal is to have at least half of your test results within the target range.

Many meters can use a computer for downloading blood glucose readings. You can download at home, or your diabetes care team can do it for you. If your blood glucose readings are frequently too high (hyperglycemia) or too low (hypoglycemia), your team can help you get back on track.

Food Planning. Of all the care skills, food planning is of primary importance to any diabetes treatment plan, because what, when and how much you eat directly affects your blood glucose levels. A diabetes food plan usually includes three meals per day, and it may or may not include snacks, depending on personal preferences. You don't have to eat special foods, and there is no special diabetes diet. Just take a look at the recipes in this book, and you'll see that meal planning when you have diabetes can be both delicious and easy!

If you've met with a registered dietitian, the two of you probably developed a customized food plan. Important considerations include your food likes and dislikes, your daily schedule, what kind of job you have and other lifestyle factors that affect eating and physical activity.

The key to success with your food plan is learning to "count" carbohydrate. Carbohydrate is found in starches (such as bread and cereal), fruits, milk and starchy vegetables (such as potatoes and squash). These foods are an important part of a nutritious diet, and they provide the glucose your body needs for energy. Carbohydrate foods also make your blood glucose levels go up unless the glucose is used, so you need to balance your intake with activity and diabetes medication in order to ensure that glucose gets into your body's cells. Carbohydrate counting helps you do this. For more information about carbohydrate counting, see page 11, or make an appointment to see a dietitian. (If you count food exchanges, see page 12.)

Physical Activity. One of the most beneficial things you can do for yourself is to find the physical activity that's right for you—and commit to it. Exercise helps lower high blood pressure, improve blood cholesterol levels and control weight. For people with diabetes, there is an added benefit: Regular physical activity helps lower blood glucose levels by making the body's cells more sensitive to insulin. And for people at risk for diabetes, exercise can even help prevent the disease from developing.

Physical activity is always an important part of diabetes treatment. In type 2 diabetes, exercise can greatly enhance blood glucose control, with or without the help of diabetes medications. In type 1 diabetes, it's necessary to plan and sometimes make adjustments for physical activity, because it can actually cause blood glucose levels

to go too low when significant insulin is circulating. But that's no reason not to exercise! There are many ways to incorporate exercise safely. See page 27 for resources that can help you learn how.

 ## 3. Emotional Health

It's sometimes easy to forget that your emotional health is just as important to your overall well-being as your physical health. The two go hand in hand. When you feel good about yourself emotionally, you tend to feel better physically. When you take care of your body, you often feel better emotionally.

Having emotional thoughts and feelings about diabetes is normal, just as it would be with any disease. Feelings such as *denial* ("If I stop thinking about it, maybe it will go away"), *fear* ("What will happen to me?") and *anger* ("It's not fair that I have diabetes") are common. *Guilt* ("If I had eaten better, then I wouldn't have gotten diabetes"), *sadness* ("I feel so bad about this") and *frustration* ("*Now* what do I have to do? This is so hard!") also are normal.

Fortunately, bolstered by a little insight and knowledge, you also can feel *relief* ("It could be worse"), *hopefulness* ("I can care for my body and my diabetes"), *adaptation* ("I don't like it, but I'll deal with it") and, finally, *acceptance* ("I have diabetes, but I'm still going to enjoy my life").

Blood Glucose Target Levels

Test Time	Target Range	Normal Range
Before meals	70–140 mg/dL	70–110 mg/dL
2 hours after start of meals	Less than 160 mg/dL	Less than 140 mg/dL
Bedtime	100–140 mg/dL	Less than 120 mg/dL

Used with permission from International Diabetes Center, Minneapolis, MN

Nurses and dietitians who specialize in diabetes care are often certified as experts in the field (often designated by "CDE," or Certified Diabetes Educator). They help people with diabetes and their families to understand:

- **What diabetes is**
- **How glucose and insulin work together to provide energy**
- **How food and activity affect blood glucose levels**
- **Different diabetes medications and how they work**
- **The purpose, importance and how-to's of daily self-care (see next section)**

Instead of thinking about diabetes as the worst thing that could happen to you, view diabetes as a wake-up call that can lead to healthier living and a longer life. Even small changes, practiced over a long time, can be a big help on the road to better health.

If you take care of your emotional self, you can come to accept diabetes as one part—and not all—of your life. This doesn't happen overnight. So give yourself the time and patience needed to work through any feelings you experience. Look to family, friends and mental health professionals if you feel you need help, and ask for it. It will be better for you and for the people who love you.

Take time to congratulate yourself on maintaining good blood glucose levels and other accomplishments. It's easy to focus too much on areas that still need work and forget to notice all the successes. Perhaps you've worked up to exercising four times a week, and you feel great. Or all of a sudden, you find that your craving for sweets has gone away! Maybe your latest achievement is much smaller—you've made it through a whole week without being so tired. Even small accomplishments deserve to be celebrated.

Diabetes Treatment

Diabetes knowledge, self-care skills and emotional support provide the foundation for your treatment plan and help support appropriate medical therapies. Food planning and physical activity are important components of care. For certain people, medications are sometimes needed as well.

 ### 1. Blood Glucose Control

The number one goal of diabetes care is to keep your blood glucose levels as close to normal as possible. Every member of your care team has a role in helping you to achieve this goal. A big part of your role is to test your blood glucose as recommended by your health-care provider. Be sure you receive and understand your self-tested blood glucose targets. You need to have a target for before meals and a target for two hours after the start of meals (post-meal blood glucose). Common times and targets for blood glucose tests are shown on page 26. Self-testing your blood glucose is critical for monitoring and managing daily control.

Hemoglobin A1c. There is a laboratory test today that shows your average blood glucose over the past two to three months. Commonly called a Hemoglobin A1c, or just A1c, it is available through any medical office and is the standard measure for evaluating overall blood glucose control. It's the best indicator of your risk for developing diabetes complications. If you have not had an A1c, be sure to talk with your health-care provider about it. It's recommended that people with diabetes have an A1c every three to four months. As for blood glucose self-tests, the goal is to keep your A1c as close to normal as possible. See the Diabetes Care Schedule on page 26 for A1c and other diabetes care targets.

The best plan for you. Your treatment plan is based on what your body needs. Anyone with type 1 diabetes needs to take insulin injections coordinated with a personalized food plan, activity and lifestyle needs. Individuals with type 2 diabetes may or may not need medication; sometimes a personalized food plan along with increased physical activity is enough to control blood glucose levels. But over time, or even right at diagnosis if warranted, your health-care professional may recommend adding a diabetes medication. You may need oral medication, insulin or both to keep your blood glucose level in target. It's important to note that diabetes medications alone cannot replace the benefits of following your food plan and staying physically active. Healthy eating and exercising dramatically improve the effectiveness of medications.

Diabetes medications. There are two types of diabetes medication: *oral medications* and *insulin injections.* All people with type 1 diabetes need to take insulin injections coordinated with a personalized food plan and with their activity and lifestyle needs. People with type 2 diabetes may need oral medications or insulin when a food plan and increased activity are not enough to keep blood glucose levels in target.

Oral medications may also be called *glucose-lowering pills, diabetes pills* or *oral agents.* There are two main types of oral agents: those that stimulate or push the pancreas to make more insulin and those that help the body use insulin more efficiently. *Insulin-stimulating agents* include those that are long-acting and taken once a day, and those that are short-acting and taken before each meal. *Insulin-sensitizing agents* help the body use insulin more efficiently by reducing insulin resistance.

Oral agents may be used alone or in combination with each other. If oral agents are not effective in keeping blood glucose levels in your target range, insulin injections may be prescribed. Many people with type 2 diabetes now take both oral agents and insulin. Oral agents are generally not used for people with type 1 diabetes.

Insulin is taken by injection, usually several times per day depending on blood glucose patterns and goals for treatment. There are two classes of insulin: *short- or rapid-acting mealtime insulin* and *intermediate- or long-acting background insulin.* Rapid-acting insulin provides a burst of insulin to cover a meal that is ready to be eaten. Mealtime insulin is also called *bolus insulin.* The more carbohydrate you have in the meal, the more insulin you need to help the body use it. This prevents blood glucose from going too high after eating. Background insulin provides a continuous supply of insulin to keep blood glucose in control overnight and between meals during the day. Background insulin is also called *basal insulin.* The newest type of background insulin, taken once a day, often in the evening, can be effective in type 2 diabetes when combined with oral agents taken during the day. It is also very effective when used with rapid-acting insulin before meals for both type 1 and type 2 diabetes.

People may not want to take insulin for various reasons, most commonly because it must be taken by injection. Fortunately, the needles on syringes are now very short and thin, so that they are barely felt. Also, many people now use insulin pens, which allow the appropriate insulin dose to be quickly injected without drawing insulin from a bottle. Pens with premixed bolus insulin and background insulin in one device are another option that can make starting insulin and insulin delivery easy.

Insulin injections are *the* most effective method of lowering blood glucose levels offered today, and studies show that most people with type 2 diabetes will eventually need insulin to control blood glucose levels. This is a natural result of having diabetes for a long time. It does not mean that the person has somehow failed or that their diabetes is getting worse. It is simply that the pancreas is making less insulin over time and treatment needs to change to match the body's needs.

2. Blood Lipids (Fats) Control

Diabetes increases your risk for heart and blood vessel disease. High blood lipids (fats) and high blood pressure add to the risk. As with blood glucose control, food planning, exercise and often medications play a crucial role in helping control these heart disease risks.

Blood lipids consist of *cholesterol* and *triglycerides*. Cholesterol and triglycerides are both made in the body and are found in food. Most of the cholesterol in the bloodstream is actually made in the body. Triglycerides come mostly from food, particularly from added fat, such as butter and salad dressing, and from sweets. Cholesterol and triglycerides are carried through the bloodstream in small packages called *lipoproteins*. There are two main lipoproteins:

- **HDL (high-density lipoprotein), or "good" cholesterol, which carries "bad" cholesterol and triglycerides out of the blood**

- **LDL (low-density lipoprotein), or "bad" cholesterol, which deposits cholesterol in blood vessel walls, narrowing the vessel opening and irritating the lining of the vessel**

To keep track of your heart health, you need to know how much HDL, LDL and triglycerides are in your blood. The only way to know this is to have your doctor order a complete cholesterol profile for you every year. Blood for this test needs to be drawn first thing in the morning before you eat. It's good to have high HDL levels and low LDL levels in your blood.

Increasing physical activity is the best way to improve HDL. Eating a healthy diet that is low in saturated fat is the best way to lower LDL and triglycerides. Target goals for cholesterol and triglycerides are on the Diabetes Care Schedule (page 26).

3. Blood Pressure Control

High blood pressure puts extra strain on your heart and in the large blood vessels in the brain and legs. It can also damage small blood vessels in the eyes and kidneys. It adds to the risk for heart disease, stroke, visual impairment, kidney disease and other diabetes complications. Blood pressure is recorded as two numbers. The upper number is the systolic blood pressure, the pressure when your heart is contracting. The lower number is the diastolic pressure, the pressure when your heart is relaxed. If either number is high, your risk for heart disease is increased. Make sure your blood pressure is checked at every health-care visit, and ask to see the results. Target goals for blood pressure are on the Diabetes Care Schedule (page 26). Making food choices that are lower in sodium has been shown to help reduce blood pressure. The maximum recommendation for daily sodium intake is 2400 milligrams if you have high blood pressure.

4. Prevent & Manage Complications

Long-term complications are caused by extended periods of high blood glucose levels, which damage small and large blood vessels. Damage to small blood vessels causes problems with the nerves (neuropathy), eyes (retinopathy) and kidneys (nephropathy). This is called *microvascular disease.* The walls of large blood vessels can be damaged by lipid buildup, high blood pressure and inflammation, which can lead to problems in the heart, brain and feet. This is called *macrovascular disease.*

Keeping blood glucose levels within the target range at least 50 percent of the time, as well as achieving an A1c of less than 7 percent, greatly reduces the risk of long-term complications.

Research confirms this, including data from the ten-year Diabetes Control and Complications Trial (DCCT), concluded in 1993, and the United Kingdom Prospective Diabetes Study, concluded in 1999. The DCCT showed that blood glucose control can:

- **Reduce eye disease by 76 percent**
- **Reduce kidney disease by 56 percent**
- **Reduce nerve damage by 60 percent**

Blood glucose control will likely reduce heart problems as well, but further study is needed.

Your diabetes care team members must do their part in monitoring diabetes complications by checking your feet, eyes and kidney function regularly for signs of damage. It is very important to follow the recommendations in the Diabetes Care Schedule (page 26) for tests and exams; do not allow them to be overlooked. Despite your best efforts, some complications may develop. Your best defense is to learn about any problems early so that you and your team can take action.

 ## 5. Other Care Essentials

Diabetes affects every aspect of your health and your health care. Therefore, your provider may recommend other treatments contributing to your overall well-being, including:

- **A daily aspirin to reduce the risk of heart attack**
- **Daily blood pressure medication (an ACE-inhibitor is recommended) for high blood pressure or to counteract the effects of kidney damage. (Some providers also prescribe these medications to prevent blood vessel damage.)**
- **Daily cholesterol-lowering medication (a statin is recommended) to treat high LDL cholesterol and to protect against heart damage**

Diabetes Care Schedule

The Diabetes Care Schedule summarizes the laboratory tests, medical examinations and lifestyle behaviors that contribute to achieving and maintaining your diabetes and health goals. Work with your diabetes care team to ensure that you receive the regular care that you need. Your health depends on it!

Test/Exam	Target	Frequency
Blood glucose self-tests	Before meals: 70–140 mg/dL	Before and after meals as recommended
	2 hours after start of meals: less than 160 mg/dL	
Hemoglobin A1c	Less than 7%	Every 3–6 months
Total cholesterol	Less than 200 mg/dL	Yearly
LDL cholesterol ("bad")	Less than 100 mg/dL	Yearly
HDL cholesterol ("good")	Greater than 40 mg/dL	Yearly
Triglycerides	Less than 150 mg/dL	Yearly
Urine protein (albumin/creatinine ratio)	Less than 30 mg/g Cr	Yearly
TSH (thyroid function)	0.2–5.5 μ/mL (varies by lab)	As recommended
ECG (electro-cardiogram)	Normal	As recommended
Weight check	As recommended	Every 3 months
Blood pressure	Less than 130/80	Every visit
Retinal eye exam	No signs of changes due to diabetes	Yearly
Foot exam, visual	Normal	Every visit
Foot exam, comprehensive	Normal	Yearly
Dental exam	Normal	Every 6 months
Flu vaccine	Completed	Yearly
Pneumonia vaccine (PPV)	Completed	Once for everyone and repeat as directed by physician
Diabetes education	Completed	At diagnosis and yearly by nurse and dietitian team
Review treatment plan	Completed	Every visit

Lifestyle Status	Recommendation
Smoke or use tobacco	Smoking cessation classes or prescription medications
Inactive	30 to 60 minutes of activity most days of the week (walking counts)
Overweight or obese	Lose 5 to 7 percent of total body weight to improve blood glucose control

Medication Use	Recommendation
Aspirin (thins blood and reduces inflammation of blood vessels)	Take daily after discussing with your medical team
ACE-inhibitor (blood pressure-lowering medication)	Take by prescription for hypertension, if urine protein is greater than 30 mg/g Cr, or if recommended for heart and circulation protection
Statin (cholesterol-lowering medication)	Take by prescription for high LDL ("bad") cholesterol or if recommended for heart protection

Used with permission from International Diabetes Center, Minneapolis, MN

Tap into Resources

The members of your diabetes care team are your first resource. Additional resources are also available.

International Diabetes Center offers a wealth of information on diabetes and diabetes self-care, including food planning, exercise, planning for pregnancy, gestational diabetes, diabetes prevention, depression and diabetes and much more. Visit their Web site and online bookstore at www.internationaldiabetescenter.com or call 1-888-825-6315.

International Diabetes Center publications used as resources for this book include:

> *Carbohydrate Counting for People with Diabetes*
>
> *Insulin BASICS*
>
> *Managing Type 2 Diabetes*
>
> *My Diabetes Health Record*
>
> *My Food Plan*
>
> *Pattern Control*
>
> *Sick Days, Travel, and Other Disruptions*
>
> *Staged Diabetes Management*
>
> *Type 2 Diabetes BASICS*
>
> *Type 2 Diabetes Prevention Pyramids*

The American Dietetic Association can provide customized answers to your questions about nutrition. Call them at 1-800-366-1655 to obtain a referral to a registered dietitian in your area. You can also listen to recorded messages about food and nutrition. Check out The American Dietetic Association's Web site at www.eatright.org.

The American Diabetes Association Web site at www.diabetes.org provides general information about diabetes. You can also call 1-800-DIABETES (1-800-342-2383) to request a free information packet. The American Diabetes Association also offers several books and pamphlets about diabetes. Call 1-800-232-6733 to request a catalog.

The American Association of Diabetes Educators can help you locate a diabetes educator in your area. Check their Web site at www.aadenet.org or call 1-800-338-3633.

Juvenile Diabetes Research Foundation is the world's leading nonprofit, nongovernmental funder of research dedicated to finding a cure for type 1 diabetes. The organization has more than 100 chapters and affiliates around the world that have helped raise awareness over the last three decades. To learn more about JDRF or to locate a chapter near you, visit their Web site at www.jdrf.org. Or call 1-800-533-CURE (1-800-533-2873).

Don't forget **support groups.** You can find one through hospitals, work places or your community center. Or talk to your doctor or dietitian about joining a group and ask when and where it meets. Supportive people in similar situations are often able to learn from and help each other. Over time, you may find that sharing your experiences will help someone else who is just beginning to learn about dealing with diabetes.

Chapter 1

Day-Starter Breakfasts

Starting your day with the right foods first thing in the morning provides energy, valuable nutrients and good blood glucose management. Try one of these easy recipes and you'll agree—the most important meal of the day can also be the most fun!

0
Carbohydrate Choices

Vegetables and Cheese Frittata 31

1-1½
Carbohydrate Choices

Country Ham and Asparagus Bake 32

1½

Cheesy Vegetable Strata 35

Oatmeal Pancakes with Maple-Cranberry Syrup 46

Potato, Bacon and Egg Scramble 34

2
Carbohydrate Choices

Carrot-Lemon Bread 41

Cinnamon-Raisin French Toast 36

Cranberry-Orange Scones 42

Double-Berry Muffins 40

Fruit Parfaits 50

Fruit-Topped Breakfast Bagels 48

Peach-Almond Coffee Cake 44

Smoked Salmon and Egg Wraps 30

2½
Carbohydrate Choices

Stuffed French Toast 38

Whole Wheat Waffles with Spicy Cider Syrup 49

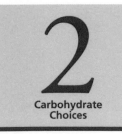

2

Carbohydrate
Choices

PREP: **10 min**

COOK: **5 min**

BAKE: **10 min**

note *from* **DR. B**

Salmon is a super source of vitamin B$_{12}$, which is needed for all body cells to function properly. Salmon also contains omega-3 fats, the good-for-you fats that are so beneficial for your heart and overall health.

"In my recent diabetes education class, Diet (Food) Exchanges never came up—we talked only about Carbohydrate Choices. I try to think of it as 'changing my eating habits' and stay away from the word diet." —PAT A.

Smoked Salmon and Egg Wraps

6 servings

6 eggs or 1 1/2 cups fat-free cholesterol-free egg product

1 tablespoon milk or water

1/4 teaspoon seasoned salt

2 tablespoons chopped fresh or 1 teaspoon dried dill weed

6 flour tortillas (8 inches in diameter)

1 package (4 1/2 ounces) smoked salmon, skinned and broken into pieces

1/2 cup finely chopped red onion

3/4 cup shredded Havarti cheese (3 ounces)

Dill weed sprigs, if desired

1 Heat oven to 350°. Line jelly roll pan, 15 1/2 × 10 1/2 × 1 inch, with aluminum foil. Beat eggs, milk and seasoned salt with fork or wire whisk until well mixed.

2 Spray 12-inch nonstick skillet with cooking spray; heat over medium heat. Pour egg mixture into skillet. As mixture begins to set at bottom and side, gently lift cooked portions with spatula so that thin, uncooked portion can flow to bottom; avoid constant stirring. Cook 3 to 4 minutes or until eggs are thickened throughout but still moist. Stir in chopped dill weed.

3 Spoon 2 to 3 tablespoons eggs down center of each tortilla. Top with salmon, onion and cheese. Fold opposite sides of each tortilla over filling (sides will not meet in center). Roll up tortilla, beginning at one of the open ends. Place wraps, seam sides down, in pan. Cover and bake about 10 minutes or until cheese is melted. Garnish with dill weed sprigs.

1 SERVING: Calories 290

Fiber 2g	Sodium 580mg
Fat 14g (Saturated 6g)	Protein 18g
Cholesterol 230mg	Carbohydrate 26g

Food Exchanges: 2 Starch; 2 Medium-Fat Meat

"I really enjoy having a frittata for an indulgent breakfast. Best of all, it's a low-carb option! Counting carbs is my life, and it's refreshing to have a low-carb selection that satisfies my morning hunger!" —KATE D.

Vegetables and Cheese Frittata

PREP: **10 min**
COOK: **14 min**

6 servings

8 eggs or 2 cups fat-free cholesterol-free egg product

1/2 teaspoon salt

1/8 teaspoon pepper

1/2 cup shredded Swiss cheese (2 ounces)

2 tablespoons canola oil or butter

2 medium bell peppers, chopped (2 cups)

1 medium onion, chopped (1/2 cup)

1 Beat eggs, salt and pepper in medium bowl with fork or wire whisk until well mixed. Stir in cheese; set aside.

2 Heat oil in ovenproof 10-inch nonstick skillet over medium heat. Cook bell peppers and onion in oil, stirring occasionally, until onion is tender. Pour egg mixture over pepper mixture. Cover and cook over medium-low heat 8 to 10 minutes or until eggs are set and light brown on bottom.

3 Set oven control to broil. Broil frittata with top 4 to 6 inches from heat about 2 minutes or until golden brown. Cut into wedges.

note from **DR. B**
Because blood glucose levels can vary at different times of the day, test your blood glucose throughout the day, not just in the morning. Good times to check it are before lunch or two hours after dinner.

1 SERVING: Calories 190

Fiber 1g	Sodium 330mg
Fat 14g (Saturated 4g)	Protein 12g
Cholesterol 300mg	Carbohydrate 5g

Food Exchanges: 1 1/2 Medium-Fat Meat; 1 Vegetable

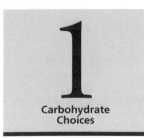

1

Carbohydrate
Choices

PREP: **20 min**

BAKE: **25 min**

STAND: **5 min**

note from **DR. B**

An easy way to cut calories is to use low-fat or fat-free dairy products, which contain half the calories of regular-fat dairy products. You can use reduced-fat Cheddar cheese in this easy recipe.

"My husband developed diabetes twenty years ago, and my daughter twelve years ago. It became clear to us as we were planning meals that the best thing for diabetes is simple, balanced, healthy eating. It's good for our whole family."

—MARY E.

Country Ham and Asparagus Bake

8 servings

1 1/2 cups chopped fully cooked ham

1 medium onion, chopped (1/2 cup)

1/4 cup chopped bell pepper

1 package (10 ounces) frozen asparagus or broccoli cuts

8 eggs or 2 cups fat-free cholesterol-free egg product

2 cups fat-free (skim) milk

1 cup all-purpose flour

1/4 cup grated Parmesan cheese

1/2 teaspoon salt

1/2 teaspoon pepper

1/2 teaspoon dried tarragon leaves

1 cup shredded Cheddar cheese (4 ounces)

1 Heat oven to 425°. Generously grease bottom and sides of rectangular baking dish, 13 × 9 × 2 inches, with shortening or cooking spray. Sprinkle ham, onion, bell pepper and frozen asparagus in baking dish.

2 Beat eggs, milk, flour, Parmesan cheese, salt, pepper and tarragon with fork or wire whisk in medium bowl until smooth; pour over ham mixture.

3 Bake uncovered about 20 minutes or until knife inserted in center comes out clean. Sprinkle with Cheddar cheese. Bake 3 to 5 minutes or until cheese is melted. Let stand 5 minutes before cutting.

1 SERVING: Calories 290

Fiber 1g	Sodium 780mg
Fat 14g	
(Saturated 7g)	Protein 22g
Cholesterol 250mg	Carbohydrate 19g

Food Exchanges: 2 Medium-Fat Meat; 1 Vegetable; 1 Starch; 1 Fat

Country Ham and Asparagus Bake

PREP: **10 min**

COOK: **10 min**

Betty's **success tip**

A breakfast of eggs, potatoes and bacon can still fit in your life; the key is moderation and counting carbohydrates. At only 1 1/2 Carbohydrate Choices, this easy recipe is perfect for breakfast, brunch or even dinner. Add a green or orange vegetable, a slice of whole wheat bread and glass of milk to round up to 4 Choices.

"My usual breakfast is oatmeal—but I know that if I increase my insulin slightly, I can enjoy this hearty weekend breakfast!"
—TIM H.

Potato, Bacon and Egg Scramble

5 servings

1 pound small red potatoes (6 or 7), cubed

6 eggs or 1 1/2 cups fat-free cholesterol-free egg product

1/3 cup fat-free (skim) milk

1/4 teaspoon salt

1/8 teaspoon pepper

2 tablespoons canola oil or butter

4 medium green onions, sliced (1/4 cup)

5 slices bacon, crisply cooked and crumbled

1 Heat 1 inch water to boiling in 2-quart saucepan. Add potatoes. Cover and heat to boiling; reduce heat to medium-low. Cover and cook 6 to 8 minutes or until potatoes are tender; drain.

2 Beat eggs, milk, salt and pepper with fork or wire whisk until well mixed; set aside.

3 Heat oil in 10-inch skillet over medium-high heat. Cook potatoes in oil 3 to 5 minutes, turning potatoes occasionally, until light brown. Stir in onions. Cook 1 minute, stirring constantly.

4 Pour egg mixture over potato mixture. As egg mixture begins to set at bottom and side, gently lift cooked portions with spatula so that thin, uncooked portion can flow to bottom; avoid constant stirring. Cook 3 to 4 minutes or until eggs are thickened throughout but still moist. Sprinkle with bacon.

1 SERVING: Calories 250

Fiber 2g	Sodium 310mg
Fat 14g (Saturated 6g)	Protein 12g
Cholesterol 270mg	Carbohydrate 21g

Food Exchanges: 1 Starch; 1 High-Fat Meat; 1 Vegetable; 1 Fat

"I know that my husband will be able to eat this strata without raising his blood sugar very much, because it's a mix of protein and carbohydrates with fiber from the vegetables. I can also count on everyone else in the family to enjoy this classic favorite for brunch."
—MICHELE H.

Cheesy Vegetable Strata

8 servings

8 slices bread

1 bag (1 pound) frozen broccoli, green beans, pearl onions and red peppers (or other combination), thawed and drained

2 cups shredded reduced-fat Cheddar cheese (8 ounces)

8 eggs or 2 cups fat-free cholesterol-free egg product

4 cups fat-free (skim) milk

1 teaspoon ground mustard

1/2 teaspoon salt

1/4 teaspoon black pepper

1/4 teaspoon ground red pepper (cayenne)

1 Cut each bread slice diagonally into 4 triangles. Arrange half of the bread triangles in ungreased rectangular pan, 13 × 9 × 2 inches. Top with vegetables. Sprinkle with cheese. Top with remaining bread.

2 Beat remaining ingredients with hand beater or wire whisk until well mixed; pour evenly over bread. Cover and refrigerate at least 2 hours but no longer than 24 hours.

3 Heat oven to 325°. Cover and bake 30 minutes. Uncover and bake about 45 minutes longer or until knife inserted in center comes out clean. Let stand 10 minutes before cutting.

1½ Carbohydrate Choices

PREP:	15 min
CHILL:	2 hr
BAKE:	1 hr 15 min
STAND:	10 min

Betty's success tip

Part of living with diabetes is planning meals. This recipe helps with the planning part in a big way because the strata can be put together the evening before and then baked in the morning. It's a make-ahead dish that's ready to bake without any last-minute fuss.

1 SERVING: Calories 245

Fiber 2g	Sodium 600mg
Fat 9g (Saturated 3g)	Protein 21g
Cholesterol 220mg	Carbohydrate 22g

Food Exchanges: 1 Starch; 2 Medium-Fat Meat; 1 Vegetable

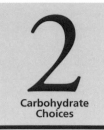

2
Carbohydrate
Choices

PREP: **5 min**
COOK: **16 min**

note *from* **DR. B**

Look for sugar-free syrup at the grocery store; the carbohydrate content is lower than regular sugar. If it's 20 calories or less per serving, it's a "free" food for you!

Cinnamon-Raisin French Toast

4 servings

2 eggs plus 1 egg white or 3/4 cup fat-free cholesterol-free egg product

3/4 cup fat-free (skim) milk

1 tablespoon sugar

1/2 teaspoon vanilla

8 slices cinnamon-raisin bread

1 Beat eggs, milk, sugar and vanilla with hand beater until smooth; pour into shallow bowl.

2 Spray griddle or 10-inch skillet with cooking spray; heat griddle to 375° or heat skillet over medium heat. Dip bread into egg mixture, coating both sides. Cook about 4 minutes on each side or until golden brown.

1 SLICE: Calories 210

Fiber 2g	Sodium 270mg
Fat 5g (Saturated 1g)	Protein 10g
Cholesterol 110mg	Carbohydrate 33g

Food Exchanges: 2 Starch; 1 Lean Meat

Stopping the Epidemic

As diabetes continues to grow worldwide, medical experts have been tackling an important question: Can diabetes be prevented? For type 1 diabetes, researchers are studying what triggers the immune system to attack the pancreas and how to stop it. For type 2 diabetes, efforts at early prevention and detection are key. Regular screenings are recommended for everyone over age 45 and for younger people with two or more risk factors. Lifestyle changes also make a difference.

Over 90 percent of the 17 million people with diabetes in the United States have type 2 diabetes, and one-third don't even know it. Half of the people diagnosed with type 2 already have a complication of diabetes on the day of diagnosis, such as numbness, tingling or pain in the feet (due to nerve damage) or early damage of the blood vessels in the eyes, leading to poor vision.

What if your blood glucose test is higher than normal but not high enough to be diabetes? Or what if you've had gestational diabetes? How can you keep from developing diabetes later in life? Studies show that making modest lifestyle changes can cut your risk of developing diabetes by at least one-half. Certain medications may also reduce your risk.

Lifestyle changes make a difference:

- Get 30 to 60 minutes, five days a week, of mild aerobic exercise such as brisk walking. (See page 123 for more on exercise.)

- Lose 5 to 7 percent of your starting weight. Losing even ten to fourteen pounds—and keeping it off—can be a significant benefit.

- Eat less total fat, particularly saturated fat.

- Increase your intake of whole grains and fiber.

Get the whole family involved. Incorporating positive habits into kids' lives early—at home and in school—makes diabetes prevention more effective. Diabetes screening and lifestyle changes offer hope that fewer people will have to live with diabetes in the future. Now, that's a goal worth striving for!

Diabetes Risk Factors

- **Family history of type 2 diabetes**

- **Being overweight**

- **Inactivity**

- **Abnormal blood cholesterol profile**

- **High blood pressure**

- **Belonging to an ethnic minority group**

- **Polycystic ovary syndrome (PCOS) affects childbearing-age women and may go undetected until they seek attention for infertility or irregular menstrual cycles. The underlying cause is insulin resistance.**

- **History of gestational diabetes or a baby weighing more than 9 pounds at birth (see page 8 for more on gestational diabetes).**

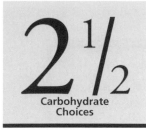

2¹/₂
Carbohydrate
Choices

PREP: **15 min**
COOK: **6 min**

"For my sweet tooth, this recipe caught my eye and appetite! You'll love this one on a late Sunday morning with a cup of fresh coffee!"
—MICHELLE M.

Stuffed French Toast

6 servings

**12 slices French bread,
1/2 inch thick**

**6 tablespoons fat-free
soft cream cheese**

**1/4 cup preserves or jam
(any flavor)**

**4 egg whites, 2 eggs or
1/2 cup fat-free cholesterol-
free egg product, slightly
beaten**

1/2 cup fat-free (skim) milk

2 tablespoons sugar

1 Spread one side of 6 slices bread with 1 tablespoon of the cream cheese. Spread one side of remaining slices with 2 teaspoons of the preserves. Place bread with cream cheese and bread with preserves together in pairs.

2 Beat egg whites, milk and sugar with wire whisk until smooth; pour into shallow bowl.

3 Spray griddle or skillet with cooking spray; heat griddle to 325° or heat skillet over medium-low heat. Dip each side of sandwich into egg mixture. Cook sandwiches 2 to 3 minutes on each side or until golden brown.

2 SLICES: Calories 205

Fiber 2g	Sodium 410mg
Fat 2g (Saturated 0g)	Protein 9g
Cholesterol 0mg	Carbohydrate 40g

Food Exchanges: 2 Starch;
1/2 Skim Milk

Stuffed French Toast

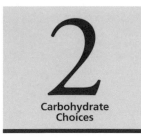

"You can't have too many good recipes for muffins—they are great to have on hand when you feel like snacking and you want to make good choices. I always try to keep some muffins in the freezer for quick breakfasts or snacks."

—SHERRY L.

PREP: **15 min**

BAKE: **25 min**

note from **DR. B**

Researchers looked at forty different fruits, vegetables and juices to measure which contained the most antioxidant capabilities. Guess what? Blueberries took home the blue ribbon.

Double-Berry Muffins

12 muffins

1/4 cup packed brown sugar

1/2 teaspoon ground cinnamon

1 cup fat-free (skim) milk

1/4 cup unsweetened applesauce

2 tablespoons canola or vegetable oil

1/2 teaspoon vanilla

1 egg or 1/4 cup fat-free cholesterol-free egg product

2 cups all-purpose flour

1/3 cup granulated sugar

3 teaspoons baking powder

1/2 teaspoon salt

1/2 cup fresh or frozen (thawed and drained) raspberries

1/2 cup fresh or frozen (thawed and drained) blueberries

1 Heat oven to 400°. Line 12 medium muffin cups (2 1/2 × 1 1/4 inches) with paper baking cups or grease bottoms only with shortening. Mix brown sugar and cinnamon; set aside.

2 Beat milk, applesauce, oil, vanilla and egg in large bowl with fork or wire whisk. Stir in flour, granulated sugar, baking powder and salt all at once just until flour is moistened (batter will be lumpy). Fold in raspberries and blueberries. Divide batter evenly among muffin cups. Sprinkle brown sugar mixture evenly over tops of muffins.

3 Bake 20 to 25 minutes or until golden brown. Immediately remove from pan to wire rack. Serve warm if desired.

1 MUFFIN: Calories 155

Fiber 1g	Sodium 240mg
Fat 3g (Saturated 1g)	Protein 3g
Cholesterol 20mg	Carbohydrate 30g

Food Exchanges: 1 Starch; 1 Fruit; 1/2 Fat

Carrot-Lemon Bread

2
Carbohydrate
Choices

PREP: **20 min**
BAKE: **1 hr 10 min**
COOL: **1 hr 15 min**

1 loaf (16 slices)

1 1/2 cups Fiber One cereal

2 2/3 cups all-purpose flour

1/3 cup granulated sugar

1/3 cup packed brown sugar

2 teaspoons baking powder

2 teaspoons pumpkin pie spice

1/2 teaspoon salt

1/2 teaspoon baking soda

1/2 cup chopped walnuts

1/3 cup lemon juice

1/4 cup canola or vegetable oil

1 teaspoon grated lemon peel

2 eggs or 1/2 cup fat-free cholesterol-free egg product

2 cans (8 ounces each) julienne-cut carrots, undrained

1 Heat oven to 350°. Grease bottom and sides of loaf pan, 9 × 5 × 3 inches, with shortening. Place cereal in plastic bag or between sheets of waxed paper; finely crush with rolling pin (or crush cereal in blender or food processor); set aside.

2 Mix flour, sugars, baking powder, pumpkin pie spice, salt and baking soda in large bowl. Stir in cereal and walnuts.

3 Beat remaining ingredients with spoon until well mixed. Stir into cereal mixture just until moistened. Pour into pan. Bake about 1 hour 10 minutes or until toothpick inserted in center comes out clean.

4 Cool 15 minutes; remove from pan to wire rack. Cool completely, about 1 hour, before slicing.

note from **DR. B**

At 4 grams per slice, this bread is a great source of fiber. Fiber can help with blood glucose management. Fruits, vegetables and whole grains, along with beans and legumes, contain high amounts of fiber.

1 SLICE: Calories 185

Fiber 4g	Sodium 230mg
Fat 7g (Saturated 1g)	Protein 4g
Cholesterol 25mg	Carbohydrate 32g

Food Exchanges: 2 Starch; 1 Fat

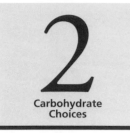

"Now that I've learned about Carbohydrate Choices, I try to focus on foods or recipes with 2 Choices or less per serving. That way, I can have more than one carbohydrate food per meal."

—PAT A.

PREP: **20 min**

BAKE: **9 min**

COOL: **5 min**

Cranberry-Orange Scones

12 scones

Betty's **success tip**

For a breakfast that stays with you through the morning, try a well-rounded meal of 3 to 4 Carbohydrate Choices that's high in complex carbohydrates and contains some protein and fat. These scones, along with a glass of milk and a fresh fruit, fit the bill.

2 cups Basic 4 cereal or other whole wheat flake cereal with cranberries

1 cup all-purpose flour

1/4 cup packed brown sugar

2 teaspoons baking powder

1 teaspoon grated orange peel

1/4 teaspoon salt

1/4 cup firm butter or margarine

1/2 cup dried cranberries

1 egg, slightly beaten, or 1/4 cup fat-free cholesterol-free egg product

1/4 cup orange artificially sweetened low-fat yogurt

Orange Glaze (below)

1 Heat oven to 400°. Place cereal in plastic bag or between sheets of waxed paper; slightly crush with rolling pin; set aside.

2 Mix flour, brown sugar, baking powder, orange peel and salt in medium bowl. Cut in butter, using pastry blender or crisscrossing 2 knives, until mixture looks like coarse crumbs. Stir in cereal, cranberries, egg and yogurt until soft dough forms.

3 Place dough on lightly floured surface. Gently roll in flour to coat; shape into ball. Pat dough into 8-inch circle with floured hands. Cut circle into 12 wedges with sharp knife dipped in flour. Place wedges about 1 inch apart on ungreased cookie sheet.

4 Bake 7 to 9 minutes or until edges are light brown. Immediately remove from cookie sheet to wire rack (place rack on waxed paper to catch glaze drips). Cool 5 minutes; drizzle with Orange Glaze. After glaze is set, store tightly covered.

Orange Glaze

1/2 cup powdered sugar

1/4 teaspoon grated orange peel

2 to 3 teaspoons orange juice

Mix all ingredients until thin enough to drizzle.

1 SCONE: Calories 170

Fiber 2g   Sodium 220mg

Fat 5g

(Saturated 3g)   Protein 3g

Cholesterol   Carbohydrate
30mg   30g

Food Exchanges: 1 Starch; 1 Fruit; 1/2 Fat

Cranberry-Orange Scones and
Watermelon-Kiwi-Banana Smoothie (page 66)

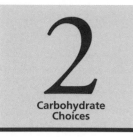

2

Carbohydrate
Choices

note from **DR. B**

Studies have shown that occasionally eating a small handful of nuts (about 1/4 cup) does not cause weight gain. It may be because the satisfaction provided by the fat in the nuts makes people eat less overall.

"I'm glad to have a recipe I can share with guests and know they will like. I not only watch my sugar intake, I also keep track of total carbohydrates."

—SHERRY L.

Peach-Almond Coffee Cake

10 servings

2/3 cup fat-free (skim) milk

1 egg or 1/4 cup fat-free cholesterol-free egg product

2 tablespoons canola or vegetable oil

1/2 teaspoon almond extract

2 cups Reduced Fat Bisquick

1/3 cup sugar

1 cup chopped fresh or frozen (thawed and drained) peaches

1/2 cup artificially sweetened vanilla low-fat yogurt

1/4 cup packed brown sugar

1/4 cup sliced almonds

1 Heat oven to 375°. Spray round pan, 8 × 1 1/2 inches, with cooking spray. Mix milk, egg, oil and almond extract in large bowl until smooth. Stir in Bisquick and sugar until Bisquick is moistened (batter will be lumpy). Spread batter in pan.

2 Mix peaches and yogurt; spoon onto batter. Swirl lightly with knife. Sprinkle with brown sugar and almonds.

3 Bake 25 to 30 minutes or until toothpick inserted in cake near center comes out clean. Serve warm or cool. Store covered in refrigerator.

1 SERVING: Calories 200

Fiber 1g

Fat 6g
(Saturated 1g)

Cholesterol
20mg

Sodium
290mg

Protein 4g

Carbohydrate
33g

Food Exchanges: 1 Starch;
1 Fruit; 1 Fat

20 Great 1-Carbohydrate-Choice Snacks

Having great snacks readily available is a valuable key to following your meal plan. Keep these on hand and reach for them whenever you need a quick, healthy snack. Each one counts as 1 Carbohydrate Choice.

- 1 granola bar, 1 ounce

- 3 graham cracker squares with 1 tablespoon of peanut butter

- 3 cups popped popcorn (no fat added) with seasoned salt

- 6 animal crackers

- 10 seasoned mini-rice or mini-popcorn cakes

- 15 mini-pretzel twists dipped in 1 tablespoon of cheese sauce

- 10 to 15 tortilla chips (1 ounce) with 1/4 cup salsa

- 4 or 5 whole-grain snack crackers or 4 to 6 saltine cracker squares plus 1 ounce of reduced-fat cheese

- 3/4 cup mix-and-match unsweetened cereals

- 1 small muffin or 3-inch cookie

- 1/2 cup sugar-free pudding

- 1 cup artificially sweetened hot cocoa

- 1 medium apple, orange or pear

- 12 to 15 cherries or grapes

- 1/4 cup raisins or other dried fruit

- 3 cups baby carrots, broccoli, cauliflower, cherry tomatoes, celery, cucumber, pea pods, bell peppers, radishes, tomatoes or zucchini with 1 tablespoon of dip

- 1 1/2 cups tomato or vegetable juice

- 1/2 cup light ice cream or 1 ice-cream bar

- 3/4 to 1 cup yogurt, artificially sweetened or plain

- 1 cup soy milk

"Just like pancakes flip, blood sugars can flip in the wrong direction quickly! To avoid trouble, it is important to know how your body reacts and to know your symptoms. Share your symptoms with people who are around you."

—KATE D.

note from **DR. B**

Oatmeal is 100 percent whole grain; using it in baked goods adds fiber and texture. Recent studies have revealed that eating 1 cup of cooked oatmeal two to four times per week has been linked to a reduction in risk for type 2 diabetes.

Oatmeal Pancakes with Maple-Cranberry Syrup

12 servings

Maple-Cranberry Syrup (below)

1/2 cup quick-cooking or old-fashioned oats

1/4 cup all-purpose flour

1/4 cup whole wheat flour

3/4 cup buttermilk

1/4 cup fat-free (skim) milk

1 tablespoon sugar

2 tablespoons canola or vegetable oil

1 teaspoon baking powder

1/2 teaspoon baking soda

1/2 teaspoon salt

1 egg or 1/4 cup fat-free cholesterol-free egg product

1 Make Maple-Cranberry Syrup; keep warm. Beat remaining ingredients with hand beater or wire whisk just until smooth. (For thinner pancakes, stir in additional 2 to 4 tablespoons milk.)

2 Spray griddle or 10-inch nonstick skillet with cooking spray; heat griddle to 375° or heat skillet over medium heat. For each pancake, pour slightly less than 1/4 cup batter from cup or pitcher onto hot griddle.

3 Cook pancakes until puffed and dry around edges. Turn; cook other sides until golden brown. Serve with syrup.

Maple-Cranberry Syrup

1/2 cup artificially-sweetened maple-flavored syrup

1/4 cup whole berry cranberry sauce

Heat ingredients in 1-quart saucepan over medium heat, stirring occasionally, until cranberry sauce is melted.

1 PANCAKE WITH SYRUP:
Calories 170

Fiber 1g	Sodium 480mg
Fat 7g (Saturated 1g)	Protein 5g
Cholesterol 35mg	Carbohydrate 23g

Food Exchanges: 1 1/2 Starch; 1/2 Fat

Oatmeal Pancakes with Maple-Cranberry Syrup

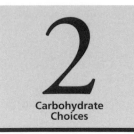

2

Carbohydrate
Choices

Fruit-Topped Breakfast Bagels

4 servings

Betty's **success tip**

Most fruits contain about the same amount of carbohydrate, so any fresh fruits can be used in place of the ones listed here. Try chopped melon, apple or any berries.

1/3 cup diced banana

1/3 cup chopped fresh or canned (drained) peaches in juice

1/3 cup fresh raspberries

1/4 cup orange or vanilla artificially sweetened low-fat yogurt

2 bagels, split

1 tablespoon prepared cinnamon-sugar

1 Mix banana, peaches, raspberries and yogurt.

2 Toast bagels. Sprinkle cinnamon-sugar evenly over warm bagel halves. Top each bagel half with 1/4 cup fruit mixture.

1 SERVING: Calories 135

Fiber 2g	Sodium 160mg
Fat 1g	
(Saturated 0g)	Protein 4g
Cholesterol 0mg	Carbohydrate 29g

Food Exchanges: 1 Starch; 1 Fruit

"I have tried to change my way of thinking about portions. It doesn't say anywhere that I have to eat a whole waffle. For me, a half-waffle with a sausage patty and half of a banana is a great low-carbohydrate meal." —PAT A.

Whole Wheat Waffles with Spicy Cider Syrup

12 servings

Spicy Cider Syrup (below)

2 eggs or 1/2 cup fat-free cholesterol-free egg product

2 cups whole wheat flour

1/4 cup canola oil or butter, melted

1 3/4 cups fat-free (skim) milk

1 tablespoon sugar

3 teaspoons baking powder

1/2 teaspoon salt

6 tablespoons wheat germ

PREP: **10 min**

BAKE: **5 min per waffle**

1 Make Spicy Cider Syrup; keep warm. Spray nonstick waffle iron with cooking spray; heat waffle iron. Beat eggs in medium bowl with hand beater until fluffy. Beat in remaining ingredients except wheat germ just until smooth.

2 For each waffle, pour about one-third of the batter from cup or pitcher onto center of hot waffle iron; sprinkle with 2 tablespoons wheat germ. (Waffle irons vary in size; check manufacturer's directions for recommended amount of batter.) Close lid of waffle iron.

3 Bake about 5 minutes or until steaming stops. Carefully remove waffle. Serve with syrup.

Spicy Cider Syrup

1/2 cup sugar

2 tablespoons all-purpose flour

1/4 teaspoon ground cinnamon

1/4 teaspoon ground nutmeg

1 cup apple cider

1 tablespoon lemon juice

2 tablespoons butter or margarine

Mix sugar, flour, cinnamon and nutmeg in 2-quart saucepan. Stir in cider and lemon juice. Cook over medium heat, stirring constantly, until mixture thickens and boils. Boil and stir 1 minute; remove from heat. Stir in butter.

note from **DR. B**
Wheat germ, a concentrated source of vitamins, minerals and protein, has a nutty flavor. Stir wheat germ into batters for baked goods, pancakes and waffles. Or top muffins, cereal or veggies with this flavor-rich whole grain. Whole grains play an important role in overall good health. It takes 3 tablespoons of wheat germ to equal 1 Carbohydrate Choice, so if you use less, you don't have to count it!

1 SERVING WITH SYRUP:
Calories 220

Fiber 3g	Sodium 270mg
Fat 8g (Saturated 3g)	Protein 6g
Cholesterol 40mg	Carbohydrate 35g

Food Exchanges: 2 Starch; 1 1/2 Fat

2

Carbohydrate
Choices

PREP: **10 min**

Fruit Parfaits

2 servings

1/2 cup chopped cantaloupe

1/2 cup sliced strawberries

1/2 cup sliced kiwifruit or honeydew melon

1/2 banana, sliced

1 cup vanilla artificially sweetened low-fat yogurt

2 tablespoons sliced almonds, toasted*

1 Alternate layers of fruit and yogurt in 2 goblets or parfait glasses, beginning and ending with fruit.

2 Top with almonds.

*To toast nuts, bake uncovered in ungreased shallow pan in 350° oven about 10 minutes, stirring occasionally, until golden brown. Or cook in ungreased heavy skillet over medium-low heat 5 to 7 minutes, stirring frequently until browning begins, then stirring constantly until golden brown.

1 SERVING: Calories 160

Fiber 5g	Sodium 60mg
Fat 5g (Saturated 1g)	Protein 8g
Cholesterol 0mg	Carbohydrate 26g

Food Exchanges: 1 1/2 Fruit; 1/2 Skim Milk

Fruit Parfaits

2 Smart Snacks and Breads

Snacking is a smart way to manage blood glucose levels and to spread calories and carbohydrates over the course of the day. Here's help on planning delicious, good-for-you snacks. As long as the total carbohydrates and calories fit into your food plan, you can nibble away!

½
Carbohydrate Choices

Chipotle Black Bean Dip with Lime Tortilla Chips 55

Roasted Vegetable Dip with Baked Pita Crisps 56

Salmon-Spinach Pinwheels 59

1
Carbohydrate Choices

Chai Tea 68

Cheddar and Green Onion Biscuits 74

Crunchy Chicken Chunks with Thai Peanut Sauce 60

Gingered Caramel Dip with Fresh Fruit 54

Parmesan-Herb Breadsticks 69

Tomato-Basil Crostini 72

1½
Carbohydrate Choices

Chewy Pizza Bread 75

Hearty Multigrain Biscuits 71

Hiker's Trail Mix 62

Triple-Fruit Yogurt Smoothie 67

Veggies and Cheese Mini-Pizzas 58

2
Carbohydrate Choices

Cinnamon-Raisin Snack Mix 64

Savory Sweet Potato Pan Bread 70

Watermelon-Kiwi-Banana Smoothie 66

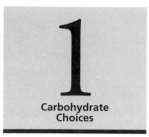

1

Carbohydrate
Choices

PREP: **10 min**

CHILL: **30 min**

Gingered Caramel Dip with Fresh Fruit

8 servings of dip (2 tablespoons each)

4 ounces reduced-fat cream cheese (Neufchâtel), softened

1/2 cup vanilla artificially sweetened low-fat yogurt

1/4 cup plus 1 to 2 teaspoons caramel topping

1 tablespoon chopped crystallized ginger

1 medium unpeeled eating apple, sliced

1 medium pear, sliced

1 medium banana, sliced (1 cup)

1 Beat cream cheese in medium bowl with electric mixer on medium speed until creamy. Beat in yogurt and 1/4 cup of the caramel topping until smooth. Cover and refrigerate at least 30 minutes until chilled.

2 Spoon dip into small serving bowl. Drizzle with 1 to 2 teaspoons caramel topping; swirl with tip of knife. Sprinkle with ginger. Serve with apple, pear and banana slices.

1 SERVING: Calories 95

Fiber 1g	Sodium 110mg
Fat 2g (Saturated 1g)	Protein 2g
Cholesterol 5mg	Carbohydrate 18g

Food Exchanges: 1/2 Starch; 1/2 Fruit; 1/2 Fat

PREP: **30 min**

STAND: **10 min**

BAKE: **25 min**

Chipotle Black Bean Dip with Lime Tortilla Chips

15 servings (2 tablespoons dip and 3 chips each)

Lime Tortilla Chips (below)

2 large dried chipotle chilies

1 cup thick-and-chunky salsa

1/2 cup jalapeño black bean dip

2 tablespoons chopped fresh cilantro

1 cup shredded Colby-Monterey Jack cheese (4 ounces)

2 medium green onions, chopped (2 tablespoons)

1 Heat oven to 350°. Make Lime Tortilla Chips.

2 Cover chilies with boiling water; let stand 10 minutes. Drain chilies and remove seeds. Chop chilies.

3 Mix chilies, salsa and bean dip; stir in cilantro. (If making ahead, cover and refrigerate up to 24 hours.) Spoon into shallow 1-quart ovenproof serving dish. Sprinkle with cheese.

4 Bake about 15 minutes or until mixture is hot and cheese is melted. Sprinkle with onions. Serve with tortilla chips.

Lime Tortilla Chips

1/2 teaspoon grated lime peel

Dash of salt

2 tablespoons lime juice

2 teaspoons olive or canola oil

2 teaspoons honey

4 flour tortillas (8 inches in diameter)

Heat oven to 350°. Spray large cookie sheet with cooking spray. Mix all ingredients except tortillas. Brush lime mixture on both sides of each tortilla. Cut each tortilla into 12 wedges. Place in single layer on cookie sheet. Bake 8 to 10 minutes or until crisp and light golden brown; cool. Store in airtight container at room temperature.

1 SERVING: Calories 95

Fiber 1g	Sodium 240mg
Fat 5g (Saturated 2g)	Protein 4g
Cholesterol 10mg	Carbohydrate 10g

Food Exchanges: 1 Starch; 1 Vegetable; 1 Fat

"This is a handy snack for those times when you need a low-carb food to ease a craving between meals. I keep the dip covered in the refrigerator, and the crisps in a covered container on the counter."
—PAT A.

PREP: **15 min**

BAKE: **30 min**

Roasted Vegetable Dip with Baked Pita Crisps

7 servings (1/4 cup dip and 3 chips each)

Betty's success tip

Dips, especially healthy ones like this, along with plenty of fun dippers make great excuses for getting together. Try dipping baby-cut carrots, cucumber slices, green bell pepper strips, toasted pita bread wedges or baked tortilla chips. This tasty dip and the easy crisps make a great choice for home entertaining or taking to your next get-together.

1 medium zucchini, sliced (2 cups)

1 medium yellow summer squash, sliced (1 1/2 cups)

1 medium red bell pepper, sliced

1 medium red onion, thinly sliced

2 cloves garlic, peeled

Cooking spray

1/2 teaspoon salt

1/4 teaspoon ground red pepper (cayenne)

Baked Pita Crisps (below)

1 Heat oven to 400°. Spread zucchini, yellow squash, bell pepper, onion and garlic in jelly roll pan, 15 1/2 × 10 1/2 × 1 inch. Spray vegetables with cooking spray. Sprinkle with salt and red pepper.

2 Bake about 30 minutes, turning vegetables once, until vegetables are tender and lightly browned.

3 Place vegetables in blender or food processor. Cover and blend on high speed about 1 minute, stopping blender occasionally to scrape sides, until smooth.

4 Serve warm, or refrigerate at least 2 hours until chilled. Serve with Baked Pita Crisps or Dippers.

Baked Pita Crisps

2 dozen pita chips

1 1/2 pita breads (6 inches in diameter)

2 teaspoons canola oil or butter, melted

1 teaspoon dried basil leaves

2 tablespoons grated Parmesan cheese

Heat oven to 375°. Split each pita bread around edge with knife to make 2 rounds. Lightly brush oil over pita rounds. Sprinkle with basil and cheese. Cut each round into 8 wedges. Place in single layer in 2 ungreased jelly roll pans, 15 1/2 × 10 1/2 × 1 inch, or on 2 cookie sheets. Bake uncovered 6 to 8 minutes or until light brown and crisp. Cool slightly (chips will continue to crisp as they cool). Serve warm or cool. Store in tightly covered container up to 3 weeks at room temperature.

1 SERVING: Calories 70

Fiber 1g	Sodium 260mg
Fat 2g (Saturated 1g)	Protein 3g
Cholesterol 0mg	Carbohydrate 11g

Food Exchanges: 1/2 Starch; 1 Vegetable

Roasted Vegetable Dip with Baked Pita Crisps

"These mini-pizzas are the perfect size to manage blood sugars! They are terrific for sporting-event snacking or for parties instead of commercial pizza delivery that tends to raise the blood sugar."
—KATE D.

PREP: **10 min**
BAKE: **7 min**

note from **DR. B**

Vegetables are loaded with the nutrients you need each day to be healthy. The Diabetes Food Guide Pyramid recommends three to five servings of veggies every day.

Veggies and Cheese Mini-Pizzas

4 servings

2 pita breads (6 inches in diameter)

4 roma (plum) tomatoes, chopped (1 cup)

2 small zucchini, chopped (2 cups)

1 small onion, chopped (1/4 cup)

2 tablespoons sliced ripe olives

1 teaspoon chopped fresh or 1/4 teaspoon dried basil leaves

1/4 cup spaghetti sauce or pizza sauce

3/4 cup shredded mozzarella cheese (3 ounces)

1 Heat oven to 425°. Split each pita bread around edge with knife to make 2 rounds. Place rounds on ungreased cookie sheet. Bake about 5 minutes or just until crisp.

2 Mix tomatoes, zucchini, onion, olives and basil. Spread spaghetti sauce evenly over rounds. Top with vegetable mixture. Sprinkle with cheese.

3 Bake 5 to 7 minutes or until cheese is melted. Cut into wedges.

---

1 SERVING: Calories 170

Fiber 3g	Sodium 370mg
Fat 5g (Saturated 3g)	Protein 10g
Cholesterol 10mg	Carbohydrate 24g

Food Exchanges: 1 Starch; 2 Vegetable; 1 Fat

1/2
Carbohydrate Choices

Salmon-Spinach Pinwheels

PREP: **15 min**

CHILL: **2 hr**

24 servings

1 package (8 ounces) reduced-fat cream cheese (Neufchâtel), softened

1 tablespoon chopped fresh or 1 teaspoon dried dill weed

4 whole wheat flour tortillas (6 inches in diameter)

1 package (4 1/2 ounces) smoked salmon, skinned and finely chopped

12 to 16 leaves fresh spinach

16 strips red bell pepper, about 5 × 1/4 inch

1 Mix cream cheese and dill weed. Spread about 1/4 cup of the cream cheese mixture over each tortilla. Sprinkle each with 1/4 cup salmon. Place 3 or 4 spinach leaves and 4 bell pepper strips evenly spaced on each tortilla.

2 Roll up tortillas tightly, spreading with additional cream cheese mixture to seal roll. Wrap securely with plastic wrap and refrigerate at least 2 hours but no longer than 24 hours.

3 To serve, cut tortilla rolls into 1-inch pieces. Place cut side up on serving platter.

note from **DR. B**
Spinach is a super source of folic acid. All cells need folic acid to function normally, but recent studies show that as many as 40 percent of Americans don't meet their folic acid requirement.

1 APPETIZER: Calories 65

Fiber 1g	Sodium 130mg
Fat 3g (Saturated 2g)	Protein 3g
Cholesterol 10mg	Carbohydrate 7g

Food Exchanges: 1/2 Starch; 1/2 Fat

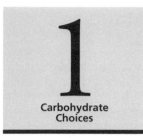
"This is my husband's favorite recipe—he prepares it with ease. We take turns making dinner, which is a huge help. I feel so lucky to have a supportive husband; his understanding since I was diagnosed with diabetes has been a lifesaver for me, because it's a daily challenge."

—MICHELLE M.

PREP: **10 min**

BAKE: **25 min**

note from **DR. B**

Rich in vitamins, minerals and heart-healthy fat, peanut butter, enjoyed in moderation, provides satisfaction. A modest amount may prevent you from overindulging on other foods.

Crunchy Chicken Chunks with Thai Peanut Sauce

8 servings

1 1/2 cups cornflakes cereal, crushed (1/2 cup)

1/2 cup Original Bisquick

3/4 teaspoon paprika

1/4 teaspoon salt

1/4 teaspoon pepper

1 pound boneless, skinless chicken breasts, cut into 1-inch pieces

Cooking spray

Thai Peanut Sauce (below)

1 Heat oven to 400°. Line jelly roll pan, 15 1/2 × 10 1/2 × 1 inch, with aluminum foil.

2 Mix cereal, Bisquick, paprika, salt and pepper in 2-quart resealable plastic food-storage bag. Shake about 6 chicken pieces at a time in bag until coated. Shake off any extra crumbs. Place chicken pieces in pan. Spray with cooking spray.

3 Bake uncovered 20 to 25 minutes or until coating is crisp and chicken is no longer pink in center. Make Thai Peanut Sauce. Serve sauce with chicken.

Thai Peanut Sauce

1/2 cup plain low-fat yogurt

1/4 cup creamy peanut butter

1/2 cup fat-free (skim) milk

1 tablespoon soy sauce

1/8 teaspoon ground red pepper (cayenne), if desired

Mix all ingredients in 10-inch nonstick skillet. Cook over medium heat 3 to 4 minutes, stirring occasionally, until mixture begins to thicken.

1 SERVING: Calories 180

Fiber 0g	Sodium 440mg
Fat 7g	
(Saturated 2g)	Protein 17g
Cholesterol 35mg	Carbohydrate 13g

Food Exchanges: 1 Starch; 2 Lean Meat

Crunchy Chicken Chunks with Thai Peanut Sauce
and Veggies and Cheese Mini-Pizzas (page 58)

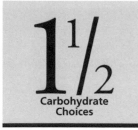

1 1/2

Carbohydrate
Choices

"Dried cranberries are my favorite dried fruit. Sometimes I substitute them for raisins and the candies. That way, I get maximum mileage from my dried cranberries!"

—TIM H.

Hiker's Trail Mix

12 servings (1/4 cup each)

1 1/2 cups roasted soy nuts

3/4 cup raisins

1/2 cup candy-coated chocolate candies

1 Mix all ingredients.

2 Store in resealable plastic food-storage bag or airtight container.

note from **DR. B**

Roasted soy nuts are a great snack because they're loaded with calcium and other minerals. Calcium is so important for bone density. Recent studies even show that getting enough calcium in your diet may be connected to your ability to lose weight.

1/4 CUP: Calories 165

Fiber 4g	Sodium 45mg
Fat 7g (Saturated 2g)	Protein 8g
Cholesterol 0mg	Carbohydrate 21g

Food Exchanges: 1 1/2 Fruit; 1 High-Fat Meat

Snacking Savvy

Snacks are often part of a diabetes food plan. Snacking during the day or evening provides an extra energy boost and is a good way to manage blood glucose levels and spread calories and carbohydrates over the course of the day. Remember to always carry a snack with you, especially when you exercise. The key to snacking well is to plan good-for-you, delicious snacks with total carbohydrates and calories that fit into your food plan. Consider these great "fast" snacks:

- *Whole-grain granola bars, fruit-and-grain bars, cereal snack mixes, ready-to-eat cereal and light popcorn* are good to carry. Choose whole-grain foods as 3 or more of your Carbohydrate Choices each day.

- *Fresh fruits and vegetables* provide many needed nutrients. Keep baby carrots, celery sticks, frozen grapes, bananas, apples, kiwifruit or other favorites on hand.

- *String cheese, cheese slices or chunks*—eaten with or without fresh fruit—provide necessary calcium. Whenever possible, choose the low-fat or nonfat versions.

- *Cereal and yogurt* are nutrient powerhouses. Choose a high-fiber cereal, such as Fiber One, and a light yogurt. Or layer the two for a parfait!

- *Lower-fat crackers and pretzels and baked tortilla chips* can be spread with roasted vegetable dip or salsa. If your food plan allows, enjoy with low-fat cheese or peanut butter.

- *Peanuts or roasted soy nuts* are great munchies, but their calories and fat can add up quickly. Mix with low-fat popcorn or mini pretzels, or sprinkle with savory herb blends.

- *Dried fruits* are packed with important vitamins, but they're concentrated sources of carbohydrate, so keep the portions small. Dried plums, apricots, dates and raisins are good choices. Stretch them by mixing with pretzels, low-fat popcorn or ready-to-eat cereal.

- *Whole-wheat sandwiches* of lean turkey, beef, ham, tuna or low-fat cheese make more substantial snacks. Mustard and other non-fat condiments are great add-ons, but keep the mayo to a minimum. Load them up with your favorite raw veggies.

- *Yogurt smoothies with fruit* can be a delicious treat as well as an excellent source of calcium, vitamins and other important nutrients. Blend your favorite light yogurt with cut-up fresh fruit.

- *Small low-fat cookies, cakes or miniature candy bars* may fit occasionally as a snack, but look at the food label for total number of carbohydrates per serving. Then, adjust the serving for your food plan.

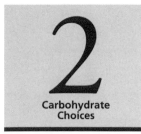

2

Carbohydrate
Choices

PREP: **5 min**

MICROWAVE: **4 min**

Betty's **success tip**

Cereals give you a lot of bang for your buck. Because cereals are fortified, cereal snacks are high in iron and other vitamins and minerals. As long as you keep track of the serving amount and watch your total carbohydrate level, you can snack away on them!

"Now that my two children with diabetes are grown, I send them 'care packages' in the mail, and many times it's a homemade snack, like this snack mix. Other good snacks to send: dried apricots, peanuts, trail mix, sugar-free hard candies or animal crackers."
— BETTY H.

Cinnamon-Raisin Snack Mix

10 servings (1/2 cup each)

1/4 cup sugar

1 teaspoon ground cinnamon

1/4 cup butter or margarine

1 1/2 cups Corn Chex cereal

1 1/2 cups Rice Chex cereal

1 1/2 cups Wheat Chex cereal

1/2 cup raisins, dried cranberries or dried cherries

1 Mix sugar and cinnamon; set aside.

2 Place butter in large microwavable bowl. Microwave uncovered on High about 40 seconds or until melted. Stir in cereals until evenly coated. Microwave uncovered 2 minutes, stirring after 1 minute.

3 Sprinkle half of the sugar mixture evenly over cereals; stir. Sprinkle with remaining sugar mixture; stir. Microwave uncovered 1 minute. Stir in raisins. Spread on paper towels to cool.

1/2 CUP: Calories 155

Fiber 1g

Fat 5g
(Saturated 3g)

Cholesterol
10mg

Sodium
190mg

Protein 2g

Carbohydrate
27g

**Food Exchanges: 1 Starch;
1 Fruit; 1 Fat**

Cinnamon-Raisin Snack Mix and Chai Tea (page 68)

2

Carbohydrate
Choices

Betty's **success tip**

Nutritious smoothies are quick and easy to grab on your way out the door. If you keep ripe bananas in the freezer, you'll always be ready for this refreshing shake.

"I know stress affects my blood sugar. This recipe helps me take a 5-minute 'mini-vacation' before or after a tough day!"

—KATE **D.**

Watermelon-Kiwi-Banana Smoothie

2 servings (1 cup each)

1 cup coarsely chopped seeded watermelon

1 kiwifruit, peeled and cut into pieces

2 ice cubes

1 ripe banana, frozen, peeled and cut into chunks

1/4 cup chilled apple juice

1 Place all ingredients in blender or food processor. Cover and blend on high speed about 30 seconds or until smooth.

2 Pour smoothie into glasses. Serve immediately.

1 SERVING: Calories 115

Fiber 3g	Sodium 5mg
Fat 1g (Saturated 0g)	Protein 1g
	Carbohydrate 29g
Cholesterol 0mg	

Food Exchanges: 2 Fruit

$1\frac{1}{2}$

Carbohydrate Choices

Triple-Fruit Yogurt Smoothie

PREP: **5 min**

4 servings (1 cup each)

2 cups vanilla artificially sweetened low-fat yogurt

1 cup fresh raspberries*

1/2 cup orange juice

1 medium banana, sliced (1 cup)

1 Place all ingredients in blender or food processor. Cover and blend on high speed about 30 seconds or until smooth.

2 Pour smoothie into glasses. Serve immediately.

1 package (10 ounces) frozen sweetened raspberries, partially thawed, can be substituted for the fresh raspberries.

Betty's **success tip**

Full of low-fat protein and calcium, yogurt— a cultured dairy product—is an excellent choice for cooking and baking. Enjoy it by itself, or use it as a low-fat ingredient in smoothies, salad dressings, dips and sauces to keep fat grams down without sacrificing flavor.

1 SERVING: Calories 105

Fiber 3g	Sodium 50mg
Fat 1g (Saturated 0g)	Protein 6g
	Carbohydrate 21g
Cholesterol 0mg	

Food Exchanges: 1 Fruit; 1/2 Skim Milk

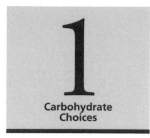

1

Carbohydrate
Choices

PREP: **5 min**

COOK: **5 min**

note *from* **DR. B**

Thanks to many advances in pre-natal care, women with diabetes can have a successful pregnancy. To make certain you get the best medical care, it is critical to see your doctor before becoming pregnant.

"I love Chai Tea and have found that I can use Earl Grey, pekoe and even herb teas in this easy recipe. Drinking this warm, soothing tea makes me feel like I am getting away from everything, even if it is for just a few minutes."

—MICHELLE M.

Chai Tea

4 servings (1 cup each)

2 cups water

4 tea bags black tea

2 cups fat-free (skim) milk

2 tablespoons honey

1/2 teaspoon ground ginger

1/2 teaspoon ground nutmeg

1/4 teaspoon ground cinnamon

1 Heat water to boiling. Add tea bags; reduce heat. Simmer 2 minutes. Remove tea bags.

2 Stir remaining ingredients into tea. Heat to boiling. Stir with wire whisk to foam milk. Pour into cups.

1 SERVING: Calories 80

Fiber 0g   Sodium 65mg

Fat 0g   Protein 4g
(Saturated 0g)
                Carbohydrate
Cholesterol   16g
0mg

Food Exchanges: 1/2 Fruit;
1/2 Skim Milk

Parmesan-Herb Breadsticks

12 breadsticks

Olive oil

Cornmeal, if desired

12 frozen whole wheat or white bread dough rolls (from 48-ounce package), thawed

2 tablespoons olive or canola oil

3 or 4 long fresh rosemary sprigs

1 tablespoon grated Parmesan cheese

1 Brush 2 cookie sheets with olive oil; sprinkle with cornmeal. Roll each ball of dough into 9-inch rope. Place ropes about 1/2 inch apart on cookie sheets.

2 Brush 2 tablespoons oil over dough. Break 36 small clusters of rosemary leaves off rosemary sprigs. Using 3 clusters for each breadstick, insert stem end of each cluster 1/4 inch deep into top of breadstick. Sprinkle cheese over dough. Cover loosely with plastic wrap and let rise in warm place about 30 minutes or until almost double.

3 Heat oven to 350°. Bake 12 to 15 minutes or until light golden brown. Serve warm.

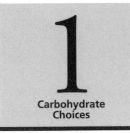

Carbohydrate Choices

PREP:	**15 min**
RISE:	**30 min**
BAKE:	**15 min**

Betty's **success tip**

A great snack by itself or with any of the soups in Chapter 6, these whole wheat and herb breadsticks can be dipped into pasta or cheese sauce. Just check the label for number of carbohydrates and convert that to Choices, using the *How Many Carbohydrate Choices?* conversion guide on page 12.

1 BREADSTICK: Calories 120

Fiber 2g

Fat 5g
(Saturated 1g)

Cholesterol 0mg

Sodium 200mg

Protein 4g

Carbohydrate 17g

Food Exchanges: 1 Starch; 1 Fat

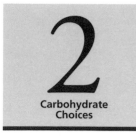

2

Carbohydrate
Choices

*"One thing I've found that really regulates my blood glucose is exercise.
Now I exercise first thing in the morning—and do I ever feel good all day!"*

—MICHELLE M.

PREP: **15 min**

BAKE: **30 min**

note from **DR. B**

**Good diabetes care
focuses on prevention
from tip to toes. So at
every doctor's visit,
remove your socks
and shoes so your
doctor can examine
your feet for any cuts,
calluses or signs of
infection.**

Savory Sweet Potato Pan Bread

10 servings

**1 1/2 cups uncooked
shredded sweet potato
(about 1/2 potato)**

1/2 cup sugar

**1/3 cup canola or
vegetable oil**

**2 eggs or 1/2 cup fat-free
cholesterol-free egg product**

1 cup all-purpose flour

1/2 cup whole wheat flour

**2 teaspoons instant minced
onion**

**1 teaspoon dried rosemary
leaves, crumbled**

1 teaspoon baking soda

1/2 teaspoon salt

1/4 teaspoon baking powder

1 tablespoon sesame seed

1 Heat oven to 350°. Grease bottom only of round pan, 9 × 1 1/2 inches, with shortening.

2 Mix sweet potato, sugar, oil and eggs in large bowl. Stir in remaining ingredients except sesame seed. Spread in pan. Sprinkle sesame seed over batter.

3 Bake 25 to 30 minutes or until toothpick inserted in center comes out clean. Serve warm.

1 SERVING: Calories 215

Fiber 2g

Fat 9g
(Saturated 1g)

Cholesterol
40mg

Sodium
470mg

Protein 4g

Carbohydrate
31g

Food Exchanges: 2 Starch;
1 1/2 Fat

Hearty Multigrain Biscuits

PREP: **10 min**
BAKE: **12 min**

10 biscuits

3/4 cup whole wheat flour

1/2 cup all-purpose flour

1/2 cup cornmeal

3 teaspoons baking powder

1/2 teaspoon salt

1/4 cup shortening

1/2 cup quick-cooking or old-fashioned oats

About 3/4 cup fat-free (skim) milk

1 Heat oven to 450°. Mix flours, cornmeal, baking powder and salt in large bowl. Cut in shortening, using pastry blender or crisscrossing 2 knives, until mixture looks like fine crumbs. Stir in oats. Stir in just enough milk so dough leaves side of bowl and forms a ball.

2 Place dough on lightly floured surface. Knead lightly 10 times. Roll or pat 1/2 inch thick. Cut with floured 2 1/2-inch round cutter. Place on ungreased cookie sheet about 1 inch apart for crusty sides, touching for soft sides. Brush with milk and sprinkle with oats if desired.

3 Bake 10 to 12 minutes or until golden brown. Immediately remove from cookie sheet. Serve warm.

Betty's **success tip**

These tasty biscuits contain three different grains: cornmeal, whole wheat and oatmeal. Combining grains adds flavor, texture and fiber, plus variety, to your eating plan.

1 BISCUIT: Calories 150

Fiber 2g	Sodium 270mg
Fat 6g (Saturated 1g)	Protein 4g
Cholesterol 0mg	Carbohydrate 21g

Food Exchanges: 1 1/2 Starch; 1 Fat

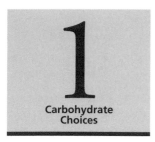

Carbohydrate Choices

PREP: **15 min**

BAKE: **8 min**

note from **DR. B**

For your next doctor appointment, bring a three-day food record. This gives the doctor important information about your meal and snack times and food selections. If you add your self-tested blood glucose numbers to the record, the information becomes even more useful.

"I really feel like I'm making something special and healthy for my family when I use fresh tomatoes from my garden. This recipe, which goes together in a snap, gives me a taste of summer."
—BETTY H.

Tomato-Basil Crostini

12 servings

12 slices Italian bread, 1/2 inch thick

1/4 cup olive or canola oil

1 large tomato, chopped (1 cup)

3 tablespoons chopped fresh basil leaves

1 tablespoon large capers or chopped ripe olives

1/2 teaspoon salt

1/2 teaspoon pepper

12 slices (1 ounce each) mozzarella cheese

1 Heat oven to 375°. Place bread slices on ungreased cookie sheets. Drizzle 1 teaspoon oil over each bread slice.

2 Mix tomato, basil, capers, salt and pepper. Spread half of the tomato mixture over bread slices; top each with cheese slice. Spread remaining tomato mixture over cheese.

3 Bake about 8 minutes or until bread is hot and cheese is melted. Serve hot.

1 SERVING: Calories 175

Fiber 1g	Sodium 380mg
Fat 10g (Saturated 4g)	Protein 10g
Cholesterol 15mg	Carbohydrate 12g

Food Exchanges: 1 Starch; 1 High-Fat Meat

Tomato-Basil Crostini and Chipotle Black Bean
Dip with Lime Tortilla Chips (page 55)

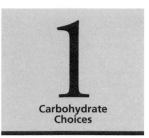

Carbohydrate Choices

Cheddar and Green Onion Biscuits

8 biscuits

1 1/3 cups all-purpose flour

1 1/2 teaspoons baking powder

1/2 teaspoon salt

1/4 teaspoon baking soda

1/4 teaspoon ground mustard

4 medium green onions, sliced (1/4 cup)

1/2 cup shredded reduced-fat Cheddar cheese (2 ounces)

3/4 cup buttermilk

3 tablespoons canola or vegetable oil

1 Heat oven to 450°. Spray cookie sheet with cooking spray. Mix flour, baking powder, salt, baking soda and mustard in medium bowl. Stir in onions and cheese.

2 Mix buttermilk and oil; stir into flour mixture until soft dough forms. Drop dough by 8 spoonfuls onto cookie sheet.

3 Bake 9 to 11 minutes or until golden brown. Serve warm.

1 BISCUIT: Calories 140

Fiber 1g	Sodium 340mg
Fat 6g (Saturated 1g)	Protein 5g
Cholesterol 5mg	Carbohydrate 18g

Food Exchanges: 1 Starch; 1 Fat

Chewy Pizza Bread

1½ Carbohydrate Choices

PREP: **10 min**
BAKE: **20 min**

8 servings (2 squares each)

1 1/2 cups all-purpose flour

1 1/2 teaspoons baking powder

1/2 teaspoon salt

3/4 cup regular or nonalcoholic beer

1/2 cup spaghetti sauce

1/3 cup shredded low-fat mozzarella cheese

Chopped fresh basil leaves, if desired

1 Heat oven to 425°. Spray square pan, 8 × 8 × 2 inches, with cooking spray. Mix flour, baking powder and salt in medium bowl. Stir in beer just until flour is moistened. Spread dough in pan. Spread spaghetti sauce over dough. Sprinkle with cheese.

2 Bake 15 to 20 minutes or until toothpick inserted in center comes out clean. Sprinkle with basil. Cut into 2-inch squares. Serve warm.

Betty's **success tip**

This bread also makes a great dipper for pizza or pasta sauce. Instead of cutting into squares, just slice into long, thin "fingers" that are easier to dip. Pass individual small bowls of sauce to make dipping easier.

1 SERVING: Calories 130

Fiber 1g

Fat 2g
(Saturated 1g)

Cholesterol 5mg

Sodium 340mg

Protein 4g

Carbohydrate 24g

Food Exchanges: 1 1/2 Starch

3 Family-Pleasing Poultry and Fish

Besides tasting great and adding variety, chicken, turkey and fish are packed with protein, which your body needs for growth and maintenance. Protein doesn't raise your blood sugar, so including foods with protein in each meal helps balance the carbohydrates you eat.

0-½
Carbohydrate Choices

Caramelized-Garlic Chicken 79

Crab Scramble Casserole 107

Halibut with Lime and Cilantro 96

—— ½ ——

Cheesy Chicken Skillet Dinner 80

Grilled Fish with Jicama Salsa 95

Honey-Mustard Turkey with Snap Peas 94

Parmesan-Dijon Chicken 78

Spinach-Shrimp Salad with Hot Bacon Dressing 104

1-1½
Carbohydrate Choices

Baked Chicken and Rice with Autumn Vegetables 88

Caribbean Chicken Salad 90

Chicken and Cantaloupe Salad 91

Chicken and Green Beans with Rice 83

Chicken Enchiladas 86

Cornmeal-Crusted Catfish 98

Kung Pao Noodles and Chicken 82

Orange-Almond Trout 101

Orange- and Ginger-Glazed Turkey Tenderloins 92

—— 1½ ——

Fajita Pizza 87

Lemony Fish over Vegetables and Rice 99

Salmon and Couscous Bake 100

2-2½
Carbohydrate Choices

Calypso Shrimp with Black Bean Salsa 105

Seafood and Vegetables with Rice 106

—— 2½ ——

Easy Mexican Chicken and Beans 84

3
Carbohydrate Choices

Italian Shrimp Stir-Fry 102

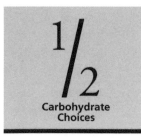

1/2

Carbohydrate
Choices

PREP: **5 min**

BAKE: **25 min**

note from **DR. B**

To reduce fat and calories, trim all visible fat from meat and remove chicken skin before cooking.

"I don't crave fried chicken anymore since this recipe's such a great substitute—the seasoning really kicks up the flavor!"
—TIM H.

Parmesan-Dijon Chicken

6 servings

3/4 cup dry bread crumbs

1/4 cup grated Parmesan cheese

1/4 cup canola oil or butter, melted

2 tablespoons Dijon mustard

6 boneless, skinless chicken breast halves (about 1 3/4 pounds)

1 Heat oven to 375°. Grease bottom and sides of rectangular pan, 13 × 9 × 2 inches, with shortening.

2 Mix bread crumbs and cheese in large resealable plastic food-storage bag. Mix oil and mustard in shallow dish. Dip chicken into oil mixture, then shake in bag to coat with crumb mixture. Place in pan.

3 Bake uncovered 20 to 25 minutes, turning once, until juice of chicken is no longer pink when centers of thickest pieces are cut.

1 SERVING: Calories 285

Fiber 0g	Sodium 440mg
Fat 14g (Saturated 3g)	Protein 30g
Cholesterol 7mg	Carbohydrate 10g

Food Exchanges: 1/2 Starch; 4 Lean Meat

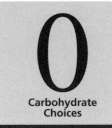

Caramelized-Garlic Chicken

5 servings

4 cloves garlic, finely chopped

1 tablespoon canola oil or butter

2 teaspoons packed brown sugar

1/4 teaspoon salt

1 pound boneless, skinless chicken breast halves

1/4 cup water

4 slices tomato

4 ounces Havarti or Swiss cheese, cut into 1/8-inch slices

1 tablespoon chopped fresh or 1/2 teaspoon dried basil leaves

1 Cook garlic and oil in 10-inch nonstick skillet over medium-low heat 1 to 2 minutes, stirring constantly, just until garlic begins to turn brown. Stir in brown sugar until melted.

2 Sprinkle salt over chicken. Add chicken to skillet. Cook 3 to 5 minutes, turning once, until brown. Add water. Cook over medium heat 8 to 10 minutes, turning once, until chicken is glazed and no longer pink when centers of thickest pieces are cut and liquid has evaporated. Chicken will be golden brown. Watch carefully to prevent scorching.

3 Top each chicken piece with tomato, cheese and basil. Cover and heat 1 to 2 minutes or until cheese is melted.

Betty's **success tip**

If you serve this chicken on toasted kaiser rolls for a great sandwich, you'll increase your Carbohydrate Choices to only 2 1/2. Add a salad or vegetable and a glass of milk, and chances are, you'll still be within your meal plan.

1 SERVING: Calories 240

Fiber 0g

Fat 13g
Saturated 7g;

Cholesterol 90mg

Sodium 330mg

Protein 27g

Carbohydrate 4g

Food Exchanges: 4 Lean Meat; 1 Vegetable

PREP: **10 min**

COOK: **10 min**

Cheesy Chicken Skillet Dinner

6 servings

1 teaspoon canola or vegetable oil

1 1/4 pounds boneless, skinless chicken breasts, cut into 3/4-inch pieces

2 large carrots, cut into 1/8-inch slices (2 cups)

1 medium zucchini, cut into 1/8-inch slices (2 cups)

2 tablespoons soy sauce

8 medium green onions, sliced (1/2 cup)

2 cups shredded sharp reduced-fat Cheddar cheese (8 ounces)

1 Heat 12-inch nonstick skillet over medium-high heat. Add oil; rotate skillet to coat bottom. Add chicken; stir-fry 4 to 5 minutes or until no longer pink in center. Remove from skillet.

2 Add carrots and zucchini to skillet; stir-fry 4 to 5 minutes or until crisp-tender. Add chicken and soy sauce; toss until chicken and vegetables are coated with soy sauce.

3 Sprinkle with onions and cheese. Cover skillet until cheese is melted.

1 SERVING: Calories 285

Fiber 2g	Sodium 600mg
Fat 16g (Saturated 8g)	Protein 31g
Cholesterol 95mg	Carbohydrate 6g

Food Exchanges: 4 Lean Meat; 1 Vegetable; 1 Fat

Cheesy Chicken Skillet Dinner

1
Carbohydrate
Choices

"To help ward off the complications of heart disease, I substitute 'lite' soy sauce in this recipe because it has less sodium than traditional soy sauce." —KATE D.

PREP: **5 min**

COOK: **15 min**

Kung Pao Noodles and Chicken

6 servings

2 cups uncooked fine egg noodles (3 ounces)

1 tablespoon canola or vegetable oil

1 1/4 pounds boneless, skinless chicken breasts, cut into 1-inch pieces

1 envelope (7/8 ounce) hot and spicy kung pao chicken Oriental seasoning mix

3/4 cup water

1 tablespoon sugar

1 tablespoon soy sauce

6 medium green onions, cut into 1-inch pieces

1/2 cup dry-roasted peanuts

Crushed red pepper, if desired

1 Cook and drain noodles as directed on package; keep warm.

2 Heat oil in 12-inch nonstick skillet over medium-high heat. Cook chicken in oil 4 to 5 minutes, stirring occasionally, until no longer pink in center.

3 Stir seasoning mix (dry), water, sugar and soy sauce into chicken. Heat to boiling. Stir in onions. Boil 30 seconds to 1 minute, stirring constantly, until sauce is thickened. Stir in noodles; toss to coat.

4 Sprinkle with peanuts and red pepper.

1 SERVING: Calories 275

Fiber 2g	Sodium 1040mg
Fat 12g (Saturated 2g)	Protein 26g
Cholesterol 70mg	Carbohydrate 18g

Food Exchanges: 1 Starch; 3 Lean Meat

1
Carbohydrate Choices

PREP: **10 min**
BAKE: **50 min**

Chicken and Green Beans with Rice

4 servings

2 cups cut-up cooked chicken

2 cups cooked rice

1/2 teaspoon salt

1/4 teaspoon pepper

2 medium stalks celery, sliced (1 cup)

1 medium onion, chopped (1/2 cup)

1 can (14 ounces) chicken broth

1 package (9 or 10 ounces) frozen cut green or yellow wax beans, thawed

1 Heat oven to 350°. Butter 2-quart casserole. Mix all ingredients in casserole.

2 Cover and bake 45 to 50 minutes or until beans are tender.

note from **DR. B**
Do you drink enough water? At least eight to ten glasses of water and other liquids daily are recommended. Beverages such as milk and herb teas also count, but remember to quench your thirst with plenty of plain water, as well.

1 SERVING: Calories 270

Fiber 3g   Sodium
                         840mg
Fat 6g
(Saturated 4g)   Protein 17g

Cholesterol   Carbohydrate
60mg   20g

Food Exchanges: 1 Starch; 2 Very Lean Meat; 1 Vegetable

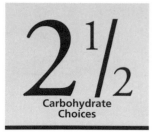

2 1/2
Carbohydrate
Choices

PREP: **8 min**
COOK: **20 min**

"I'm trying hard to lose weight, and I've found that even a couple hundred calories a day makes a difference. Besides having a pretty good calorie count, this recipe has a lot of fiber, and I just feel better when I know I'm eating food that's good for me."
—SHERRY L.

Easy Mexican Chicken and Beans

4 servings

1 pound boneless, skinless chicken breast strips for stir-fry

1 envelope (1 1/4 ounces) taco seasoning mix

1 can (15 to 16 ounces) black or pinto beans, rinsed and drained

1 can (11 ounces) whole kernel corn with red and green peppers, undrained

1/4 cup water

1 Spray 10-inch nonstick skillet with cooking spray. Cook chicken in skillet over medium-high heat 8 to 10 minutes, stirring occasionally, until no longer pink in center.

2 Stir in seasoning mix, beans, corn and water. Cook over medium-high heat 8 to 10 minutes, stirring frequently, until sauce is slightly thickened. Serve with tortillas.

1 SERVING: Calories 335

Fiber 12g	Sodium 780mg
Fat 5g (Saturated 1g)	Protein 37g
Cholesterol 70mg	Carbohydrate 48g

Food Exchanges: 2 1/2 Starch; 4 Very Lean Meat

Easy Mexican Chicken and Beans

PREP: **20 min**

BAKE: **25 min**

note from **DR. B**

**Chicken and turkey
are good sources of
zinc, a mineral that
you need in trace
amounts. Deficiencies
of zinc can lead to
decreased appetite
and a reduced ability
to taste and smell.**

Chicken Enchiladas

6 servings

**1 cup mild green sauce
(salsa verde) or salsa**

1/4 cup cilantro sprigs

1/4 cup parsley sprigs

1 tablespoon lime juice

2 cloves garlic

**2 cups chopped cooked
chicken or turkey**

**3/4 cup shredded mozzarella
cheese (3 ounces)**

**6 flour tortillas (6 to 8 inches
in diameter)**

**1 medium lime,
cut into wedges**

1 Heat oven to 350°. Spray rectangular baking dish,
11 × 7 × 1 1/2 inches, with cooking spray. Place green
sauce, cilantro, parsley, lime juice and garlic in blender
or food processor. Cover and blend on high speed about
30 seconds or until smooth. Reserve half of mixture.

2 Mix remaining sauce mixture, the chicken and 1/4 cup of
the cheese. Spoon about 1/4 cup chicken mixture onto each
tortilla. Roll tortilla around filling; place seam side down in
baking dish.

3 Pour reserved sauce mixture over enchiladas. Sprinkle with
remaining 1/2 cup cheese. Bake uncovered 20 to 25 minutes
or until hot. Serve with lime wedges.

1 SERVING: Calories 210

Fiber 2g   Sodium
                  420mg
Fat 8g
(Saturated 3g)   Protein 20g

Cholesterol   Carbohydrate
50mg   17g

Food Exchanges: 1 Starch;
2 1/2 Lean Meat

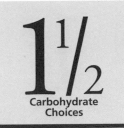

PREP: **18 min**
BAKE: **12 min**

Fajita Pizza

6 servings

2 tablespoons canola or vegetable oil

1/2 pound boneless, skinless chicken breasts, cut into 1/8- to 1/4-inch strips

1/2 medium bell pepper, cut into thin strips

1 small onion, sliced

1/2 cup salsa or picante sauce

1 1/2 cups Original Bisquick

1/3 cup very hot water

1 1/2 cups shredded mozzarella cheese (6 ounces)

1 Move oven rack to lowest position. Heat oven to 450°. Grease 12-inch pizza pan with shortening or butter.

2 Heat 10-inch skillet over medium-high heat. Add oil; rotate skillet to coat bottom and side. Cook chicken in oil 3 minutes, stirring frequently. Stir in bell pepper and onion. Cook 3 to 4 minutes, stirring frequently, until vegetables are crisp-tender and chicken is no longer pink in center; remove from heat. Stir in salsa; set aside.

3 Stir Bisquick and very hot water until soft dough forms; beat vigorously with spoon 20 strokes. Press dough in pizza pan, using fingers dipped in Bisquick; pinch edge to form 1/2-inch rim. Sprinkle 3/4 cup of the cheese over crust. Top with chicken mixture. Sprinkle with remaining 3/4 cup cheese.

4 Bake about 12 minutes or until crust is golden brown and cheese is melted and bubbly.

Betty's **success tip**

Get the family involved! Making a meal together not only gets the job done quickly, it allows you to spend time together, and kids are more likely to eat what they've pre-pared. Young children can set the table and wash vegetables. Older children can shred cheese, cut up vegetables and assemble recipes.

1 SERVING: Calories 295

Fiber 1g	Sodium 690mg
Fat 15g (Saturated 5g)	Protein 19g
Cholesterol 40mg	Carbohydrate 22g

Food Exchanges: 1 Starch; 2 Medium-Fat Meat; 1 Fat; 1 Vegetable

1
Carbohydrate
Choices

PREP: **20 min**
BAKE: **30 min**

"The good news is that the foods that are good for my husband with diabetes are good for our whole family."
—MICHELE **H.**

Baked Chicken and Rice with Autumn Vegetables

5 servings

1 package (about 6 ounces) chicken-flavored rice mix or 1 package (6.9 ounces) chicken-flavored rice and vermicelli mix

2 cups 1-inch pieces butternut squash

1 medium zucchini, cut lengthwise in half, then crosswise into 3/4-inch slices

1 medium red bell pepper, cut into 1-inch pieces (1 cup)

4 boneless, skinless chicken breast halves (about 1 1/4 pounds)

2 cups water

1/2 cup garlic-and-herb spreadable cheese

1 Heat oven to 425°. Mix rice, contents of seasoning packet, squash, zucchini and bell pepper in ungreased rectangular pan, 13 × 9 × 2 inches.

2 Spray 10-inch skillet with cooking spray; heat over medium-high heat. Cook chicken in skillet about 5 minutes, turning once, until brown. Remove chicken from skillet.

3 Add water to skillet; heat to boiling. Pour boiling water over rice mixture; stir to mix. Stir in cheese. Place chicken on rice mixture.

4 Cover and bake about 30 minutes or until liquid is absorbed and juice of chicken is no longer pink when centers of thickest pieces are cut.

1 SERVING: Calories 240

Fiber 2g	Sodium 360mg
Fat 7g (Saturated 3g)	Protein 27g
Cholesterol 70mg	Carbohydrate 19g

Food Exchanges: 1 Starch; 3 Lean Meat; 1 Vegetable

Baked Chicken and Rice with Autumn Vegetables

1

Carbohydrate
Choices

PREP: **10 min**
COOK: **12 min**

note from **DR. B**

Though protein won't raise your blood glucose levels, it's still wise to eat only one serving per meal to control your total calorie and fat intake.

"A cool supper for a hot summer night: meat, vegetables and fruit all in one bowl. I keep a bag of ready-to-eat breadsticks in my freezer to accompany this salad."

—BETTY H.

Caribbean Chicken Salad

4 servings

1 pound boneless, skinless chicken breasts, cut into 1/2-inch strips

2 tablespoons blackened seasoning blend

1 tablespoon canola or vegetable oil

1 package (5 ounces) mixed baby salad greens (4 cups)

1 medium mango, peeled, pitted and diced (1 cup)

1/2 medium red onion, sliced (3/4 cup)

1 small red bell pepper, chopped (1/2 cup)

2/3 cup fruit-flavored vinaigrette

1 Place chicken in heavy-duty resealable plastic food-storage bag. Sprinkle seasoning blend over chicken; seal bag and shake until chicken is evenly coated.

2 Heat oil in 10-inch nonstick skillet over medium-high heat. Cook chicken in oil 10 to 12 minutes, stirring frequently, until no longer pink in center. Remove chicken from skillet; drain on paper towels.

3 Toss salad greens, mango, onion and bell pepper in large bowl; divide among 4 plates. Top with chicken. Drizzle with vinaigrette.

1 SERVING: Calories 235

Fiber 3g
Fat 7g
(Saturated 1g)
Cholesterol 70mg

Sodium 660mg
Protein 26g
Carbohydrate 20g

Food Exchanges: 3 Lean Meat; 1 Vegetable; 1 Fruit

"When buying canned fruit, determine what liquid it's packed in (natural juices or syrup), and check the carbs listed on the label. By always checking, you can keep your sugar intake low." —PAT A.

Chicken and Cantaloupe Salad

6 servings

1/4 cup plain yogurt

1/4 cup mayonnaise or salad dressing

1 tablespoon lemon juice

1 tablespoon chopped fresh chives

1/4 teaspoon salt

5 cups 1 1/2-inch pieces cantaloupe

2 1/2 cups cut-up cooked chicken

1 cup red or green grapes, cut in half

1 medium cucumber, cut into 1 × 1/4-inch strips

1 Mix yogurt and mayonnaise in large bowl. Stir in lemon juice, chives and salt.

2 Stir in remaining ingredients. Serve immediately, or refrigerate at least 2 hours until chilled but no longer than 24 hours.

Betty's **success tip**

Try combining mayonnaise and yogurt for a delightful balance. You get the creamy flavor of the mayo along with the tangy flavor and great low-fat content of the yogurt. Together, they make an excellent flavor base for this tasty salad.

1 SERVING: Calories 250

Fiber 2g	Sodium 220mg
Fat 12g (Saturated 2g)	Protein 19g
Cholesterol 5mg	Carbohydrate 18g

Food Exchanges: 2 1/2 Lean Meat; 1/2 Vegetable; 1 Fruit; 1/2 Fat

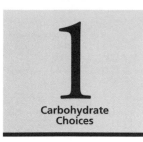

1
Carbohydrate
Choices

PREP: **3 min**
COOK: **25 min**

"Fresh ginger gives this dish a really distinctive taste. For a twist, I marinated the turkey breast in a low-fat sweet-and-sour dressing the night before, then drained and cooked as the recipe indicates."
—MICHELE H.

Orange- and Ginger-Glazed Turkey Tenderloins

4 servings

1 tablespoon canola or vegetable oil

1 pound turkey breast tenderloins

1/3 cup orange marmalade

1 teaspoon finely chopped gingerroot or 1/2 teaspoon ground ginger

1 teaspoon white or regular Worcestershire sauce

1 Heat oil in 10-inch skillet over medium heat. Cook turkey in oil about 5 minutes or until brown on one side; turn turkey.

2 Stir in remaining ingredients; reduce heat to low.

3 Cover and simmer 15 to 20 minutes, stirring occasionally, until sauce is thickened and juice of turkey is no longer pink when center of thickest piece is cut. Cut turkey into thin slices. Spoon sauce over turkey.

1 SERVING: Calories 210

Fiber 0g   Sodium 70mg

Fat 4g   Protein 26g
(Saturated 1g)
                  Carbohydrate
Cholesterol   17g
95mg

Food Exchanges: 4 Very Lean Meat; 1 Fruit

Sick Days and Travel

Any illness, even a simple cold, puts extra stress on your body, which can raise blood glucose levels. Changes to your normal routine can affect your blood glucose levels when you travel: You may be more or less active than usual, dine out more frequently or experience time zone changes. Planning ahead can help.

Sick Days

- *Check your blood glucose* every two to four hours, and record the results.

- *Keep taking your diabetes medications* even if you can't keep food down. Your body will still make glucose and you need your medicines. Call your doctor to ask if you need to change doses.

- *Drink at least one cup of water* or other sugar-free, caffeine-free liquids every hour while you're awake.

- *Eat foods with carbohydrate* such as saltine crackers, frozen pops or soup with noodles if you can't eat your usual foods. Sip on liquids like regular soda pop or juice if you can't eat.

- *Test your urine for ketones* (a buildup of acids in the blood) every two to four hours, or anytime your blood glucose is over 250 mg/dL.

Traveling

- *Always wear an ID bracelet or necklace* that states "I have diabetes," so you can get the appropriate help in an emergency.

- *Follow your food plan* as closely as possible. Carry a carbohydrate snack to prevent low blood glucose when you're active or in case a meal is delayed.

- *Keep your medicines* and blood-testing supplies in your carry-on bag when flying. Bring the original box and label for your insulin.

- *Discuss your trip* with your diabetes care team if you're traveling to another time zone or climate. Adjustments in your medication may be necessary.

- *Take extra diabetes supplies,* especially if you are going to another country. And bring comfortable shoes to keep your feet healthy while enjoying new sites.

Call Your Doctor Immediately If:

- **Most of your blood glucose readings are higher than 250 mg/dL for two days in a row**

- **You are vomiting or have persistent diarrhea**

- **Your blood glucose level falls too low more than once during your illness**

- **You have moderate to high amounts of ketones**

- **You feel sleepier than usual**

PREP: **5 min**

MARINATE: **20 min**

COOK: **15 min**

note from **DR. B**

Because this dish is made from meat and vegetables, the carbohydrate content is quite low. Add 1/3 cup of cooked rice or pasta, a slice of whole-grain bread or a dessert to round out your meal. Carbohydrates, as long as they're controlled in a diabetic diet, remain your body's favorite source of energy.

Honey-Mustard Turkey with Snap Peas

4 servings

1 pound uncooked turkey breast slices, about 1/4 inch thick

1/2 cup Dijon and honey poultry and meat marinade

1 cup baby-cut carrots, cut lengthwise in half

2 cups frozen snap pea pods

1 Place turkey in shallow glass or plastic dish. Pour marinade over turkey; turn slices to coat evenly. Cover dish and let stand at room temperature 20 minutes.

2 Spray 10-inch skillet with cooking spray; heat over medium heat. Drain most of marinade from turkey. Cook turkey in skillet about 5 minutes, turning once, until brown.

3 Add carrots, lifting turkey to place carrots on bottom of skillet. Top turkey and carrots with pea pods. Cover and cook about 7 minutes or until carrots are crisp-tender and turkey is no longer pink in center.

1 SERVING: Calories 145

Fiber 3g

Fat 1g
(Saturated 0g)

Cholesterol
75mg

Sodium
500mg

Protein 29g

Carbohydrate
10g

Food Exchanges: 3 Very Lean Meat; 2 Vegetable

"I'm trying to eat fish more often because my dietitian has encouraged me to. I do like to grill it, and this recipe has both a marinade and a salsa so it's very flavorful. The more often I eat it, the more I like it!" —SUSAN A.

PREP: **15 min**
CHILL: **2 hr**
MARINATE: **30 min**
GRILL: **10 min**

Grilled Fish with Jicama Salsa

6 servings

Jicama Salsa (below)

1 1/2 pounds swordfish, tuna or marlin steaks, 3/4 to 1 inch thick

3 tablespoons olive or canola oil

1 tablespoon lime juice

1/4 teaspoon salt

1/8 teaspoon crushed red pepper

1 Make Jicama Salsa.

2 If fish steaks are large, cut into 6 serving pieces. Mix oil, lime juice, salt and red pepper in shallow glass or plastic dish or heavy-duty resealable plastic food-storage bag. Add fish; turn to coat with marinade. Cover dish or seal bag and refrigerate 30 minutes.

3 Heat coals or gas grill for direct heat. Remove fish from marinade; reserve marinade. Cover and grill fish 5 to 6 inches from medium heat about 10 minutes, brushing 2 or 3 times with marinade and turning once, until fish flakes easily with fork. Discard any remaining marinade. Serve fish with salsa.

Jicama Salsa

2 cups chopped peeled jicama (3/4 pound)

1 medium cucumber, peeled and chopped (1 cup)

1 medium orange, peeled and chopped (3/4 cup)

1 tablespoon chopped fresh cilantro or parsley

1 tablespoon lime juice

1/2 teaspoon chili powder

1/4 teaspoon salt

Mix all ingredients in glass or plastic bowl. Cover and refrigerate at least 2 hours to blend flavors.

Betty's **success tip**

Low-fat salsas, relishes and chutneys can turn humble foods into taste sensations. Featuring the flavors of lime, orange, cucumber and jicama, this salsa adds a splash of flavor to your grilled fish.

1 SERVING: Calories 185

Fiber 3g	Sodium 190mg
Fat 10g (Saturated 2g)	Protein 20g
Cholesterol 60mg	Carbohydrate 7g

Food Exchanges: 3 Lean Meat; 1 Vegetable

"Eating fish several times a week helps me to control my blood glucose. Exercise, in conjunction with eating right, not only makes me feel better and look better, I also know I am doing the right things to stay healthy." —SHERRY L.

PREP: **10 min**

MARINATE: **15 min**

GRILL: **20 min**

note from **DR. B**

Be sure to take your medications as prescribed. If you have any questions, ask your doctor or pharmacist. Know when to take them, with what, how to store them and how to avoid side effects. Take a list of all your medications, the doses and how often you take them to each doctor visit.

Halibut with Lime and Cilantro

2 servings

Lime-Cilantro Marinade (below)

2 halibut or salmon steaks (about 3/4 pound)

Freshly ground pepper to taste

1/2 cup salsa

1 Make Lime-Cilantro Marinade in shallow glass or plastic dish or resealable plastic food-storage bag. Add fish; turn several times to coat with marinade. Cover and refrigerate 15 minutes, turning once.

2 Heat coals or gas grill for direct heat. Remove fish from marinade; discard marinade. Cover and grill fish 4 to 6 inches from medium heat 10 to 20 minutes, turning once, until fish flakes easily with fork. Sprinkle with pepper. Serve with salsa.

Lime-Cilantro Marinade

2 tablespoons lime juice

1 tablespoon chopped fresh cilantro

1 teaspoon olive or vegetable oil

1 clove garlic, finely chopped

Mix all ingredients.

1 SERVING: Calories 150

Fiber 1g

Fat 3g
(Saturated 1g)

Cholesterol 75mg

Sodium 400mg

Protein 27g

Carbohydrate 5g

Food Exchanges: 3 1/2 Very Lean Meat; 1 Vegetable

Halibut with Lime and Cilantro
and Bulgur Pilaf (page 137)

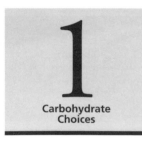

Carbohydrate Choices

PREP: **10 min**

BAKE: **15 min**

note from **DR. B**

Eating fish at least once a week is recommended by health experts because most fish is low in fat and calories and contains heart-healthy nutrients. Fattier fish, such as salmon, tuna and trout, are rich in omega-3 fatty acids that help protect the heart. Many people who have diabetes either have or are at risk for heart disease, so it's a good idea to follow these guidelines.

1 SERVING: Calories 275

Fiber 1g	Sodium 390mg
Fat 14g (Saturated 2g)	Protein 25g
Cholesterol 90mg	Carbohydrate 13g

Food Exchanges: 1 Starch; 3 Lean Meat; 1 Fat

"Relaxing times spent together as a family are priceless. Fresh fish caught from the lake makes this a family favorite at our summer cabin." —BETTY H.

Cornmeal-Crusted Catfish

4 servings

1/4 cup yellow cornmeal

1/4 cup dry bread crumbs

1 teaspoon chili powder

1/2 teaspoon paprika

1/2 teaspoon garlic salt

1/4 teaspoon pepper

1 pound catfish fillets, about 3/4 inch thick

1/4 cup ranch dressing

Chopped fresh parsley, if desired

1 Heat oven to 450°. Spray broiler-pan rack with cooking spray. Mix cornmeal, bread crumbs, chili powder, paprika, garlic salt and pepper.

2 Remove and discard skin from fish. Cut fish into 4 serving pieces. Lightly brush dressing on all sides of fish. Coat fish with cornmeal mixture. Place fish on rack in broiler pan.

3 Bake uncovered about 15 minutes or until fish flakes easily with fork. Sprinkle with parsley.

Lemony Fish over Vegetables and Rice

PREP: **10 min**

COOK: **23 min**

4 servings

1 package (6.2 ounces) fried rice (rice and vermicelli mix with almonds and Oriental seasonings)

2 tablespoons butter or margarine

2 cups water

1/2 teaspoon grated lemon peel

1 bag (1 pound) frozen corn, broccoli and red peppers (or other combination)

1 pound mild-flavored fish fillets (such as cod, flounder, sole or walleye pike), about 1/2 inch thick

1/2 teaspoon lemon pepper

1 tablespoon lemon juice

2 tablespoons chopped fresh parsley

1 Cook rice and butter in 12-inch nonstick skillet over medium heat 2 to 3 minutes, stirring occasionally, until rice is golden brown. Stir in water, seasoning packet from rice mix and lemon peel. Heat to boiling; reduce heat. Cover and simmer 10 minutes.

2 Stir in frozen vegetables. Heat to boiling, stirring occasionally. Cut fish into 4 serving pieces; arrange on rice mixture. Sprinkle fish with lemon pepper; drizzle with lemon juice. Reduce heat.

3 Cover and simmer 8 to 10 minutes or until fish flakes easily with fork and vegetables are tender. Sprinkle with parsley.

Betty's **success tip**

This simple one-pan recipe is a huge help when you need to prepare dinner in a flash. If you would rather use another vegetable combination, select one you prefer and prepare the dish the same way.

1 SERVING: Calories 230

Fiber 3g

Fat 7g
(Saturated 1g)

Cholesterol 55mg

Sodium 330mg

Protein 23g

Carbohydrate 22g

Food Exchanges: 1 Starch; 2 1/2 Lean Meat; 1 Vegetable

PREP: **12 min**

BAKE: **25 min**

note from **DR. B**

Packed with omega-3 fatty acids, salmon is low in saturated fat and high in polyunsaturated oils. Polyunsaturated fats, also found in corn oil, soybean oil and sunflower oil, are good choices because they don't tend to elevate blood cholesterol levels like saturated fat does.

Salmon and Couscous Bake

5 servings

1 pound salmon fillets, about 3/4 inch thick

1 package (5.6 ounces) toasted pine nut couscous mix

1 1/2 cups hot water

1 tablespoon olive or canola oil

1 tablespoon lemon juice

1/2 teaspoon dried dill weed

1 small zucchini, coarsely chopped

1 small yellow summer squash, coarsely chopped

1/4 teaspoon dried dill weed

Toasted pine nuts, if desired

1 Heat oven to 350°. Spray square baking dish, 8 × 8 × 2 inches, with cooking spray. Cut fish into 5 serving pieces.

2 Stir couscous, seasoning packet from couscous mix, water, oil, lemon juice, 1/2 teaspoon dill weed, the zucchini and yellow squash in baking dish. Place fish on couscous mixture. Sprinkle fish with 1/4 teaspoon dill weed.

3 Cover and bake 20 to 25 minutes or until liquid is absorbed and fish flakes easily with fork. Sprinkle with pine nuts.

1 SERVING: Calories 280

Fiber 2g	Sodium 60mg
Fat 10g (Saturated 2g)	Protein 24g
	Carbohydrate 25g
Cholesterol 60mg	

Food Exchanges: 1 1/2 Starch; 2 1/2 Lean Meat; 1 Vegetable

"Now here's a great recipe for adding more fish to everyone's diet. I've tried to pick out a couple of favorite fish recipes to use a couple of times per month."

—LORI S.

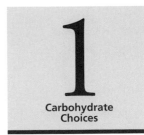

1

Carbohydrate
Choices

PREP: **10 min**
COOK: **15 min**

Orange-Almond Trout

4 servings

1 pound trout, salmon or other medium-firm fish fillets, about 3/4 inch thick

1/4 cup butter or margarine

1/4 cup sliced almonds

1 medium onion, sliced

1/2 cup all-purpose flour

1 teaspoon salt

1/2 teaspoon paprika

1/8 teaspoon pepper

2 oranges, peeled and sectioned

1 Cut fish into 4 serving pieces.

2 Melt butter in 10-inch skillet over medium heat. Cook almonds and onion in butter, stirring occasionally, until onion is tender. Remove almonds and onion with slotted spoon; keep warm.

3 Mix flour, salt, paprika and pepper. Coat fish with flour mixture. Cook fish in same skillet over medium heat 6 to 10 minutes, turning once, until fish is brown and flakes easily with fork.

4 Top fish with almonds and onion. Garnish with orange sections.

note from **DR. B**
You might ask, "Where do I start finding the right foods for my food plan?" Start with foods you like, talk it over with your dietitian and then customize your food plan from there. You may find that you don't need to modify too much as long as you're controlling carbohydrates and eating mostly low-fat, healthy foods.

1 SERVING: Calories 320

Fiber 3g	Sodium 550mg
Fat 18g (Saturated 6g)	Protein 24g
Cholesterol 75mg	Carbohydrate 19g

Food Exchanges: 3 Medium-Fat Meat; 1 Vegetable; 1 Fruit

"This recipe appeals to my teenage son. The nonmeat, low-fat and high-fiber ingredients are a plus for a weight-conscious person of any age."

—MICHELLE M.

PREP: **15 min**

COOK: **15 min**

Italian Shrimp Stir-Fry

5 servings

Betty's **success tip**

This quick and easy stir-fry was a real winner in our test kitchens. If you prefer chicken to shrimp, use 3/4 pound boneless, skinless chicken breasts, cut into 1-inch pieces. Stir-fry the chicken 3 to 4 minutes or until no longer pink in the center.

8 ounces uncooked linguine

3/4 cup reduced-calorie Italian dressing

1 1/2 teaspoons grated lemon peel

3 cloves garlic, finely chopped

3/4 pound fresh or frozen (thawed) uncooked medium shrimp, peeled and deveined

3 cups broccoli flowerets

1 medium yellow summer squash, cut lengthwise in half, then cut crosswise into slices (1 1/2 cups)

2 tablespoons water

8 cherry tomatoes, cut in half

12 extra-large pitted ripe olives, cut in half

1/4 cup chopped fresh basil leaves

Grated Parmesan cheese, if desired

1 Cook and drain linguine as directed on package; keep warm. Mix dressing, lemon peel and garlic; set aside.

2 Spray 12-inch nonstick skillet with cooking spray; heat over medium-high heat. Add shrimp; stir-fry about 2 minutes or until shrimp are pink and firm. Remove shrimp from skillet.

3 Spray skillet with cooking spray; heat over medium-high heat. Add broccoli and squash; stir-fry 1 minute. Add water. Cover and simmer about 3 minutes, stirring occasionally, until vegetables are crisp-tender (add water if necessary to prevent sticking).

4 Stir in dressing mixture; cook 30 seconds. Stir in tomatoes, olives, basil, shrimp and linguine; stir-fry until hot. Sprinkle with cheese.

1 SERVING: Calories 310

Fiber 4g

Fat 8g
(Saturated 1g)

Cholesterol 100mg

Sodium 660mg

Protein 19g

Carbohydrate 45g

Food Exchanges: 2 Starch; 1 Medium-Fat Meat; 3 Vegetable

**Italian Shrimp Stir-Fry and Cheddar and Green
Onion Biscuits (page 74)**

"I practice yoga and Pilates a couple of times every week, and they are the most rewarding exercises I do. They keep me flexible in mind, body and spirit."

—SHERRY L.

PREP: **10 min**

COOK: **10 min**

note from **DR. B**

Rather than totally eliminating fat from your diet, simply try to reduce the amount you consume and use monounsaturated and polyunsaturated fats more often. Occasionally eating a small amount of bacon and feta cheese is fine, as long as your overall food plan is lower in saturated fat.

Spinach-Shrimp Salad with Hot Bacon Dressing

4 servings

4 slices bacon, cut into 1-inch pieces

1/4 cup white vinegar

1 tablespoon sugar

1/4 teaspoon ground mustard

4 cups lightly packed bite-size pieces spinach leaves

1 cup sliced mushrooms (3 ounces)

1 cup crumbled feta cheese (4 ounces)

1/2 pound cooked peeled deveined medium shrimp, thawed if frozen

1 Cook bacon in 10-inch skillet over medium-high heat, stirring occasionally, until crisp. Stir in vinegar, sugar and mustard; continue stirring until sugar is dissolved.

2 Toss spinach, mushrooms, cheese and shrimp in large bowl. Drizzle hot bacon dressing over spinach mixture; toss to coat. Serve immediately.

1 SERVING: Calories 215

Fiber 1g	Sodium 670mg
Fat 12g (Saturated 6g)	Protein 20g
Cholesterol 150mg	Carbohydrate 7g

Food Exchanges: 1 1/2 Medium-Fat Meat; 1 Vegetable

2
Carbohydrate Choices

PREP: **20 min**
COOK: **5 min**

Calypso Shrimp with Black Bean Salsa

4 servings

1/2 teaspoon grated lime peel

1 tablespoon lime juice

1 tablespoon canola or vegetable oil

1 teaspoon finely chopped gingerroot

1 clove garlic, finely chopped

1 pound uncooked peeled deveined large shrimp, thawed if frozen

Black Bean Salsa (below)

1 Mix all ingredients except shrimp and Black Bean Salsa in medium glass or plastic bowl. Stir in shrimp; let stand 15 minutes.

2 Meanwhile, make Black Bean Salsa.

3 Cook shrimp in 10-inch skillet over medium-high heat about 5 minutes, turning once, until pink and firm. Serve with salsa.

Black Bean Salsa

1 can (15 ounces) black beans, rinsed and drained

1 medium mango, peeled, pitted and chopped (1 cup)

1 small red bell pepper, chopped (1/2 cup)

2 medium green onions, sliced (2 tablespoons)

1 tablespoon chopped fresh cilantro

1/2 teaspoon grated lime peel

1 to 2 tablespoons lime juice

1 tablespoon red wine vinegar

1/4 teaspoon ground red pepper (cayenne)

Mix all ingredients.

Betty's **success tip**

Managing diabetes is an everyday challenge. When you're feeling tired of your usual recipes, try some new and different foods to perk up your meals.

1 SERVING: Calories 255

Fiber 8g	Sodium 600mg
Fat 3g (Saturated 1g)	Protein 27g
Cholesterol 160mg	Carbohydrate 39g

Food Exchanges: 1 Starch; 3 1/2 Very Lean Meat; 1 Fruit

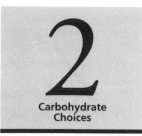
PREP: **15 min**

COOK: **10 min**

1 SERVING: Calories 240

Fiber 1g	Sodium 730mg
Fat 2g (Saturated 0g)	Protein 22g
Cholesterol 80mg	Carbohydrate 35g

Food Exchanges: 1 Starch; 2 Very Lean Meat; 1 Vegetable

Seafood and Vegetables with Rice

6 servings

1 package (8 ounces) sliced mushrooms (3 cups)

1 can (14 ounces) chicken broth

3 roma (plum) tomatoes, cut into fourths and sliced (1 1/2 cups)

1/2 cup sliced drained roasted red bell peppers (from 7-ounce jar)

1/2 pound uncooked peeled deveined small shrimp, thawed if frozen

1/2 pound cod fillets, cubed

6 ounces bay scallops

1/2 cup white wine or chicken broth

1/2 teaspoon salt

1/4 to 1/2 teaspoon red pepper sauce

1/4 cup chopped fresh cilantro

4 cups hot cooked rice

1 Heat mushrooms and broth to boiling in 3-quart saucepan. Stir in remaining ingredients except cilantro and rice. Heat to boiling; reduce heat.

2 Cover and simmer 5 to 7 minutes or until shrimp are pink and firm. Stir in cilantro. Serve in bowls over rice.

Crab Scramble Casserole

8 servings

1 tablespoon canola oil
or butter, melted

12 eggs

1/2 cup fat-free (skim) milk

1 teaspoon salt

1/2 teaspoon white pepper

1 1/2 teaspoons chopped
fresh or 1/2 teaspoon dried
dill weed

1 cup chopped cooked
crabmeat or imitation
crabmeat

1 package (8 ounces)
reduced-fat cream cheese
(Neufchâtel), cut into
1/2-inch cubes

2 medium green onions,
sliced (2 tablespoons)

Paprika

1 Pour oil into square baking dish, 8 × 8 × 2 inches; tilt dish to coat bottom. Beat eggs, milk, salt, white pepper and dill weed in large bowl with fork or wire whisk until well blended. Stir in crabmeat, cream cheese and onions. Pour into baking dish. Cover and refrigerate at least 4 hours but no longer than 24 hours.

2 Heat oven to 350°. Sprinkle paprika over egg mixture. Bake uncovered 45 to 50 minutes or until center is set.

0
Carbohydrate
Choices

PREP: **10 min**
CHILL: **4 hr**
BAKE: **50 min**

note *from* **DR. B**
Having trouble changing your eating habits? Here's a way to help yourself. Select a specific goal, such as "I will drink 1% instead of 2% milk" and write it down. You may be surprised how something so simple makes it feel real. Taking smaller, more specific steps helps you begin the process of change.

1 SERVING: Calories 205

Fiber 0g	Sodium 590mg
Fat 14g (Saturated 6g)	Protein 16g
Cholesterol 350mg	Carbohydrate 4g

Food Exchanges: 2 Medium-Fat Meat; 1 Fat

Chapter 4

Marvelous Meat

In addition to providing protein, lean cuts of beef and pork can be a great way to get the vitamins and minerals your body needs. Here are easy, all-family recipes sure to add variety and delicious choices to your eating plan.

½

Carbohydrate Choices

Breaded Pork Chops 132

Fajita Salad 120

Savory Beef Tenderloin 110

1-1½

Carbohydrate Choices

Hamburger-Pepperoni Pie 121

Honey-Mustard Pork Medallions 126

1½

Beef Medallions with Pear-Cranberry Chutney 112

Beef, Lettuce and Tomato Wraps 118

Old-Time Beef and Vegetable Stew 114

Orange Teriyaki Beef with Noodles 116

Pizza Burgers 122

Southwestern Pork Salad 130

Strip Steaks with Mango-Peach Salsa 111

2

Carbohydrate Choices

Pan-Fried Ham with Sweet Balsamic-Peach Sauce 133

Pork Tenderloin with Roasted Vegetables 124

Roasted Pork Chops and Vegetables 128

Speedy Pork Dinner 129

3

Carbohydrate Choices

Couscous and Sweet Potatoes with Pork 127

PREP: **15 min**

COOK: **10 min**

note from **DR. B**

Having beef for dinner? Beef is a super source of the mineral zinc, which is important for growth, wound healing and your ability to taste foods.

Savory Beef Tenderloin

4 servings

1 pound beef tenderloin

2 teaspoons chopped fresh or 1/2 teaspoon dried marjoram leaves

2 teaspoons sugar

1 teaspoon coarsely ground pepper

1 tablespoon canola oil or butter

1 cup sliced mushrooms (3 ounces)

1 small onion, thinly sliced

3/4 cup beef broth

1/4 cup dry red wine or nonalcoholic wine

1 tablespoon cornstarch

1 Cut beef into four 3/4-inch slices. Mix marjoram, sugar and pepper; rub on both sides of beef slices. Heat oil in 10-inch skillet over medium heat. Cook beef in oil 3 to 5 minutes, turning once, until brown. Remove beef to serving platter; keep warm.

2 Cook mushrooms and onion in drippings in skillet over medium heat about 2 minutes, stirring occasionally, until onion is crisp-tender.

3 Mix broth, wine and cornstarch; stir into mushroom mixture. Cook over medium heat, stirring constantly, until mixture thickens and boils. Boil and stir 1 minute. Pour over beef.

1 SERVING: Calories 225

Fiber 1g	Sodium 270mg
Fat 11g (Saturated 5g)	Protein 25g
Cholesterol 70mg	Carbohydrate 8g

Food Exchanges: 3 Lean Meat; 1 Vegetable

PREP: **10 min**

BROIL: **10 min**

Strip Steaks with Mango-Peach Salsa

4 servings

1/4 cup finely chopped red bell pepper

2 teaspoons finely chopped seeded jalapeño chilies

1 teaspoon finely chopped or grated gingerroot or 1/4 teaspoon ground ginger

1/4 cup peach preserves

1 tablespoon lime juice

1 medium mango, peeled, pitted and chopped (1 cup)

4 beef boneless New York strip steaks (1 pound)

1 to 2 teaspoons Caribbean jerk seasoning

1 Mix bell pepper, chilies and gingerroot in medium bowl. Stir in preserves, lime juice and mango.

2 Set oven control to broil. Sprinkle both sides of beef with jerk seasoning. Place on rack in broiler pan. Broil with tops 4 to 6 inches from heat 6 to 10 minutes, turning once, until desired doneness. Serve with salsa mixture.

note from **DR. B**
You don't have to avoid all red meat if you're trying to lose weight. By selecting lean cuts, trimming all visible fat and eating small portions, you can enjoy meat as part of a healthy diet.

1 SERVING: Calories 255

Fiber 1g	Sodium 260mg
Fat 8g (Saturated 3g)	Protein 25g
Cholesterol 65mg	Carbohydrate 22g

Food Exchanges: 3 Lean Meat; 1 1/2 Fruit

PREP: **15 min**

COOK: **23 min**

Beef Medallions with Pear-Cranberry Chutney

4 servings

1/2 large red onion, thinly sliced

2 cloves garlic, finely chopped

2 tablespoons dry red wine or grape juice

2 firm ripe pears, peeled and diced

1/2 cup fresh or frozen cranberries

2 tablespoons packed brown sugar

1/2 teaspoon pumpkin pie spice

4 beef tenderloin steaks, about 1 inch thick (1 pound)

1 Spray 12-inch skillet with cooking spray; heat over medium-high heat. Cook onion, garlic and wine in skillet about 5 minutes, stirring frequently, until onion is tender but not brown.

2 Stir in remaining ingredients except beef; reduce heat. Simmer uncovered about 10 minutes, stirring frequently, until cranberries burst. Place chutney in small bowl; set aside.

3 Cook beef in skillet over medium heat about 8 minutes for medium doneness, turning once. Serve with chutney.

1 SERVING: Calories 250

Fiber 3g   Sodium 60mg

Fat 8g   Protein 25g
(Saturated 3g)   Carbohydrate 23g

Cholesterol 65mg

Food Exchanges: 3 Lean Meat; 1 1/2 Fruit

Beef Medallions with Pear-Cranberry Chutney
and Broccoli and Tomatoes with Herbs (page 199)

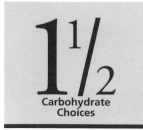

Carbohydrate Choices

"It's important to keep a daily record of your carbohydrate intake. Set your goal and stay within that range. My goal is 10 to 12 Carbohydrate Choices a day. If you're good about this on a daily basis, you can be a little careless on your birthday and a few holidays."

—PAT A.

PREP: **5 min**

COOK: **10 min**

note from **DR. B**

Developing and sticking to a schedule for monitoring blood sugar is one of the best tools you can use to learn how food and exercise affect your diabetes.

Old-Time Beef and Vegetable Stew

6 servings

1 pound lean beef boneless sirloin

1 bag (1 pound) frozen stew vegetables, thawed and drained

1 can (15 ounces) extra-thick and zesty tomato sauce

1 can (14 ounces) beef broth

2 cans (5 1/2 ounces each) spicy eight-vegetable juice

1 Cut beef into 1/2-inch cubes. Spray 10-inch nonstick skillet with cooking spray; heat over medium-high heat. Cook beef in skillet about 5 minutes, stirring occasionally, until brown.

2 Stir in remaining ingredients. Heat to boiling; reduce heat. Simmer uncovered 5 minutes, stirring occasionally.

1 SERVING: Calories 200

Fiber 3g	Sodium 860mg
Fat 5g (Saturated 1g)	Protein 19g
Cholesterol 40mg	Carbohydrate 22g

Food Exchanges: 1 Starch; 2 Lean Meat; 1 Vegetable

Calming Mind and Body

A normal part of life, stress can be positive, such as getting ready for a vacation, or it can be negative, such as losing out on a promotion. Excess negative or ongoing stress may make it harder to control blood glucose levels. Fortunately, there are ways to manage stress and diabetes at the same time.

What is stress?

Stress is the body's response to the perception that you are somehow "under attack." That feeling may arise if you sense a threat to your physical or emotional well-being or your self-esteem. When the brain senses a threat, it signals the release of stress hormones that prepare the body for "fight or flight." These stress hormones release a burst of glucose that gives the body energy to deal with the threat at hand. This can cause your blood glucose levels to rise. Stress can also cause physical reactions that make it harder to fight infection and for cells to use insulin effectively.

How can stress be prevented?

When you become stressed or don't get enough sleep, you tax your immune system and can get sick. Prevent unnecessary physical or emotional stress by taking care of yourself. Here are some ways to de-stress:

- *Get a good night's sleep*, aiming for at least six to eight hours each night.

- *Keep your individual self-management plan* first and foremost. Follow your food plan and exercise regularly so you can better manage everyday physical or emotional stress.

- *Plan your day and week* so that you can control rushing around.

- *Think positively* to prevent the body's hormonal response to stress. Some people say to themselves, "I can handle this problem. It's not as bad as it seems at first glance."

- *Talk things out* with someone when you need extra support. Find a good friend, a support group or a counselor to talk to.

- *Try **yoga***, the practice of balancing mind, body and spirit by deep breathing, stretching, strengthening and meditating; or ***progressive muscle relaxation,*** the process of tensing and relaxing muscle groups in a sequenced pattern. Both practices can help you relax.

- *Enjoy a quiet moment* of contemplation, mindfulness or meditation by closing your eyes, focusing on one thought, word, image or sound, and allowing other thoughts to float away. Meditation can provide a sense of peacefulness and inner calm.

- *Laugh out loud* to keep your spirits up. Studies show that laughter has a calming effect. Having a smile on your face makes it easier to cope with stress.

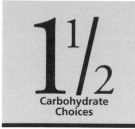
"When I first got diabetes, I didn't know if I could have Asian food with a sweet sauce. It's good to know I can!"
—Tim H.

PREP: **5 min**
COOK: **15 min**

Orange Teriyaki Beef with Noodles

4 servings

1 pound beef boneless sirloin, cut into thin strips

1 can (14 ounces) beef broth

1/4 cup teriyaki stir-fry sauce

2 tablespoons orange marmalade

Dash of ground red pepper (cayenne)

1 1/2 cups snap pea pods

1 1/2 cups uncooked fine egg noodles (3 ounces)

1 Spray 12-inch skillet with cooking spray; heat over medium-high heat. Cook beef in skillet 2 to 4 minutes, stirring occasionally, until brown. Remove beef from skillet; keep warm.

2 Add broth, stir-fry sauce, marmalade and red pepper to skillet. Heat to boiling. Stir in pea pods and noodles; reduce heat to medium. Cover and cook about 5 minutes or until noodles are tender.

3 Stir in beef. Cook uncovered 2 to 3 minutes or until sauce is slightly thickened.

1 SERVING: Calories 230

Fiber 1g	Sodium 1210mg
Fat 4g (Saturated 1g)	Protein 28g
Cholesterol 75mg	Carbohydrate 21g

Food Exchanges: 1 Starch; 3 Very Lean Meat; 1 Vegetable

Orange Teriyaki Beef with Noodles

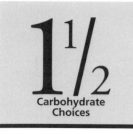
"To cut down on fat and save time, I'd skip cooking the beef and use low-fat brands of deli roast beef and mozzarella cheese instead. I find that many supermarkets carry them now."

—LORI S.

PREP: **20 min**

BROIL: **10 min**

note from **DR. B**

Broiling, braising and roasting are healthy, low-fat techniques to use when preparing meats. Grilling also allows the fat to drip away from the meat.

Beef, Lettuce and Tomato Wraps

4 servings

1 1/2 tablespoons chili powder

2 teaspoons dried oregano leaves

1 teaspoon ground cumin

1 teaspoon salt

1 pound beef top sirloin steak, about 3/4 inch thick

4 flour tortillas (6 to 8 inches in diameter)

3/4 cup reduced-fat sour cream

1 tablespoon prepared horseradish

4 cups shredded lettuce

1 large tomato, chopped (1 cup)

1 Mix chili powder, oregano, cumin and salt. Rub mixture on both sides of beef. Let stand 10 minutes at room temperature.

2 Set oven control to broil. Place beef on rack in broiler pan. Broil with top 3 to 4 inches from heat about 5 minutes on each side for medium doneness or until beef is desired doneness. Cut into 1/8-inch slices.

3 Warm tortillas as directed on package. Mix sour cream and horseradish. Spread 3 tablespoons horseradish mixture over each tortilla; top each with 1 cup of the lettuce and 1/4 cup of the tomato. Top with beef. Wrap tortillas around filling.

1 SERVING: Calories 280

Fiber 3g	Sodium 820mg
Fat 9g (Saturated 4g)	Protein 29g
Cholesterol 75mg	Carbohydrate 24g

Food Exchanges: 1 1/2 Starch; 4 Lean Meat

Beef, Lettuce and Tomato Wraps

PREP: **12 min**

COOK: **6 min**

Fajita Salad

4 servings

1 pound lean beef boneless sirloin steak

1 tablespoon canola or vegetable oil

2 medium bell peppers, cut into strips

1 small onion, thinly sliced

4 cups bite-size pieces salad greens

1/3 cup Italian dressing

1/4 cup plain yogurt

1 Cut beef with grain into 2-inch strips; cut strips across grain into 1/8-inch slices. Heat oil in 10-inch nonstick skillet over medium-high heat. Cook beef in oil about 3 minutes, stirring occasionally, until brown. Remove beef from skillet.

2 Cook bell peppers and onion in skillet about 3 minutes, stirring occasionally, until bell peppers are crisp-tender. Stir in beef.

3 Place salad greens on serving platter. Top with beef mixture. Mix dressing and yogurt; drizzle over salad.

1 SERVING: Calories 265

Fiber 3g	Sodium 250mg
Fat 15g (Saturated 2g)	Protein 26g
Cholesterol 65mg	Carbohydrate 10g

Food Exchanges: 3 Medium-Fat Meat; 2 Vegetable; 1 Fat

PREP: **20 min**
BAKE: **30 min**
STAND: **5 min**

Hamburger-Pepperoni Pie

6 servings

1 pound extra-lean
ground beef

1/3 cup dry bread crumbs

1 1/2 teaspoons chopped
fresh or 1/2 teaspoon
dried oregano leaves

1/4 teaspoon salt

1 egg or 1/4 cup fat-free
cholesterol-free egg product

1/2 cup sliced mushrooms

1 small green bell pepper,
chopped (1/2 cup)

1/3 cup chopped pepperoni
(2 ounces)

1/4 cup sliced ripe olives

1 cup spaghetti sauce

1 cup part-skim shredded
mozzarella cheese (4 ounces)

1 Heat oven to 400°. Mix beef, bread crumbs, oregano, salt and egg. Press mixture evenly against bottom and side of ungreased pie plate, 9 × 1 1/4 inches.

2 Sprinkle mushrooms, bell pepper, pepperoni and olives into beef-lined plate. Pour spaghetti sauce over toppings.

3 Bake uncovered about 25 minutes or until beef is no longer pink in center and juice is clear; carefully drain. Sprinkle with cheese. Bake about 5 minutes longer or until cheese is light brown. Let stand 5 minutes before cutting.

note *from* **DR. B**
This beef recipe is a super source of both vitamin B$_{12}$, which is important for body cells, particularly nerves, to function properly, and iron, a mineral that's vital for oxygen transfer in the blood.

1 SERVING: Calories 320

Fiber 1g	Sodium 740mg
Fat 19g (Saturated 7g)	Protein 24g
Cholesterol 95mg	Carbohydrate 14g

Food Exchanges: 3 Medium-Fat Meat; 3 Vegetable; 1 Fat

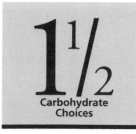

1 1/2
Carbohydrate
Choices

PREP: **5 min**

COOK: **14 min**

Betty's **success tip**

Wow! For only 1 1/2 Carbohydrate Choices, you can have this tasty burger and the bun, along with cheese and olives. Drink a glass of milk and have a fruit and a salad for a total of 4 Carbohydrate Choices.

Pizza Burgers

6 sandwiches

1 pound extra-lean ground beef

1 medium onion, chopped (1/2 cup)

1 small green bell pepper, chopped (1/2 cup)

1 jar (14 ounces) pepperoni-flavored or regular pizza sauce

1/2 cup sliced ripe olives

6 whole wheat sandwich buns, split

1 cup shredded pizza cheese blend (4 ounces)

1 Cook beef, onion and bell pepper in 10-inch skillet over medium heat 8 to 10 minutes, stirring occasionally, until beef is brown; drain.

2 Stir in pizza sauce and olives. Heat to boiling, stirring occasionally.

3 Spoon about 1/2 cup beef mixture on bottom half of each bun. Immediately sprinkle each with 2 tablespoons of the cheese; add tops of bun. Serve immediately or let stand about 2 minutes until cheese is melted.

1 SANDWICH: Calories 360

Fiber 4g

Fat 20g
(Saturated 7g)

Cholesterol 55mg

Sodium 930mg

Protein 24g

Carbohydrate 25g

Food Exchanges: 1 1/2 Starch; 2 1/2 Medium-Fat Meat; 1/2 Fat

Activity Just Feels Good

Studies show that moderate physical activity helps control diabetes and even reduces the risk of developing diabetes by more than half! If you have diabetes, 30 to 60 minutes of physical activity each day will lower your blood glucose levels. Check it out with this simple exercise: measure your blood glucose with a meter, then walk briskly for 20 minutes. Recheck your blood glucose; chances are good that it has dropped thirty to fifty points (mg/dL). Try it! Seeing a nice drop in your blood glucose may motivate you to exercise.

Even short periods of moderate aerobic exercise over the course of the day can improve your health. If you spend close to 30 minutes being physically active on most days, you're already exercising! Regular and consistent activity helps your body use insulin more effectively, not just after exercise but all day. Best of all, you'll feel great!

Countdown to a Great Workout

You're more likely to continue exercising if you choose an activity you like. To enjoy a great workout:

- *See your doctor* for an evaluation before you begin exercising. Your doctor may ask you to do a treadmill or cardiac stress test to determine how vigorously you can work out. Stretching is great for flexibility and mild weight training increases strength (and also lowers blood glucose).

- *Buy supportive shoes* and cotton socks. Examine your feet after exercising for calluses or blisters that indicate an improper fit.

- *Measure your blood glucose level* before and after exercise, and carry a carbohydrate snack with you in case your blood glucose level gets too low.

- *Get a step meter* and set your daily goal. 10,000 steps equals 5 miles!

- *Find an activity you like* whether it's walking, swimming, playing a team sport or yoga. Even better, combine a number of different activities.

- *Aim for at least 30 minutes of activity* on most days. You can portion your exercise throughout the day if that's easier for your schedule. Remember, every little bit helps!

How Active Are You?

On an average day, how many minutes do you spend:

- **Walking from the parking lot to your office, the store or a restaurant**

- **Walking up stairs and down at work or at home**

- **Walking up and down the sidelines at your child's sports event**

- **Mowing the lawn or gardening**

- **Vacuuming the floor**

- **Walking the dog**

- **Biking, dancing or playing sports**

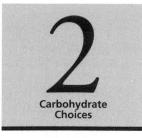

PREP: **10 min**

BAKE: **40 min**

STAND: **5 min**

Betty's **success tip**

Here's a dish that's elegant enough for company and still fits your meal plan. Even better, it all bakes in one pan for easy cleanup!

"I always keep carrot sticks, celery sticks and other good-for-me snacks on hand and ready to eat. Then I have no excuse to reach for the wrong kind of snack."
—SHERRY L.

Pork Tenderloin with Roasted Vegetables

6 servings

2 pork tenderloins (each about 3/4 pound)

1 pound baby-cut carrots

2 pounds new potatoes (16 to 20), cut in half

1 medium onion, cut into wedges

6 whole cloves garlic

1 tablespoon olive or canola oil

2 teaspoons dried rosemary leaves, crumbled

1 teaspoon dried sage leaves, crumbled

1/4 teaspoon salt

1/4 teaspoon pepper

1 Spray shallow roasting pan with cooking spray. Place pork in pan. Insert meat thermometer so tip is in thickest part of pork. Place carrots, potatoes, onion and garlic around pork. Drizzle with oil; sprinkle with rosemary, sage, salt and pepper.

2 Bake uncovered 25 to 30 minutes or until thermometer reads 155°. Remove pork from pan. Stir vegetables and continue baking 5 to 10 minutes or until tender. Cover pork and let stand 10 to 15 minutes or until thermometer reads 160° and pork is slightly pink in center. Serve pork with vegetables and garlic.

1 SERVING: Calories 310

Fiber 6g	Sodium 190mg
Fat 6g (Saturated 2g)	Protein 29g
Cholesterol 70mg	Carbohydrate 41g

Food Exchanges: 2 Starch; 3 Very Lean Meat; 1 Vegetable

Pork Tenderloin with Roasted Vegetables

Carbohydrate Choices

PREP: **10 min**
MARINATE: **15 min**
COOK: **8 min**

Betty's **success tip**

Pork has slimmed down! Once thought of as a high-fat meat, pork today is leaner than it's ever been. For the very leanest pork cut, choose the tenderloin. At only 1 Carbohydrate Choice, this would make a great dinner served with Fettuccine with Asparagus and Mushrooms (page 160) and Hearty Multigrain Biscuits (page 71).

Honey-Mustard Pork Medallions

4 servings

1 pound pork tenderloin

2 tablespoons honey

1 tablespoon yellow mustard

1/4 teaspoon salt

1/4 teaspoon ground allspice

1/8 teaspoon ground red pepper (cayenne)

1/4 cup water

2 teaspoons packed brown sugar

1 Cut pork into 1/4-inch slices. Mix remaining ingredients except water and brown sugar in shallow glass or plastic bowl. Add pork; turn to coat with marinade. Cover and refrigerate 15 minutes. Mix water and brown sugar until sugar is dissolved; set aside.

2 Spray 10-inch nonstick skillet with cooking spray; heat over medium-high heat. Remove pork from marinade; discard marinade. Cook pork in skillet 5 to 6 minutes, turning once, until no longer pink. Remove pork from skillet; keep warm.

3 Reduce heat to low. Stir water mixture into drippings in skillet. Heat to boiling; stirring constantly. Boil and stir 1 minute. Drizzle sauce over pork.

1 SERVING: Calories 190

Fiber 0g	Sodium 250mg
Fat 5g (Saturated 2g)	Protein 26g
Cholesterol 70mg	Carbohydrate 11g

Food Exchanges: 4 Very Lean Meat; 1 Fruit

3

Carbohydrate Choices

PREP: **10 min**
COOK: **10 min**

Couscous and Sweet Potatoes with Pork

5 servings

1 1/4 cups uncooked couscous

1 pound pork tenderloin, thinly sliced

1 medium sweet potato, peeled and cut into julienne strips

1 cup thick-and-chunky salsa

1/2 cup water

2 tablespoons honey

1/4 cup chopped fresh cilantro

1 Cook couscous as directed on package.

2 While couscous is cooking, spray 12-inch skillet with cooking spray. Cook pork in skillet over medium heat 2 to 3 minutes, stirring occasionally, until brown.

3 Stir sweet potato, salsa, water and honey into pork. Heat to boiling; reduce heat to medium. Cover and cook 5 to 6 minutes, stirring occasionally, until potato is tender. Sprinkle with cilantro. Serve pork mixture over couscous.

Betty's **success tip**

Want a little crunch with this quick pasta and pork dinner? Try baby-cut carrots, apple wedges, bell pepper strips or celery sticks. For dessert, try Vanilla-Cherry Crunch (page 231) or Double-Ginger Cookies (page 220); each contain only 1 Choice per serving, so at 4 Carbohydrate Choices, this dinner is well within most eating plans.

1 SERVING: Calories 325

Fiber 4g	Sodium 270mg
Fat 4g (Saturated 1g)	Protein 27g
Cholesterol 55mg	Carbohydrate 49g

Food Exchanges: 3 Starch; 2 Very Lean Meat; 1 Vegetable

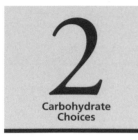

2
Carbohydrate
Choices

PREP: **20 min**
BAKE: **1 hr**

note from **DR. B**
If you find Carbohydrate Choices that don't match up exactly to the *How Many Carbohydrate Choices?* conversion guide on page 12, it's because that food or recipe is high in fiber. That's a good thing! When a food has more than 5 grams of fiber, you subtract the total grams of fiber from the total carbohydrates. Then, find that number on the conversion guide to calculate your Carbohydrate Choices.

1 SERVING: Calories 300

Fiber 5g	Sodium 170mg
Fat 7g	
(Saturated 2g)	Protein 24g
Cholesterol 55mg	Carbohydrate 40g

Food Exchanges: 2 Starch; 2 Lean Meat; 1 Vegetable

"A hearty one-dish meal—potatoes, vegetables and meat—that's great for a cold winter supper. I freeze leftovers in single servings; they're great for packed lunches or quick suppers—that really helps me plan ahead."
—BETTY **H.**

Roasted Pork Chops and Vegetables

4 servings

2 teaspoons parsley flakes

1/2 teaspoon dried marjoram leaves

1/2 teaspoon dried thyme leaves

1/2 teaspoon garlic salt

1/4 teaspoon coarsely ground pepper

4 pork rib chops, 1/2 inch thick (1 pound)

Olive oil-flavored cooking spray

6 new potatoes, cut into fourths (3 cups)

4 ounces mushrooms, cut in half (1 1/2 cups)

1 medium green bell pepper, cut into 1-inch pieces

1 medium onion, cut into thin wedges

1 medium tomato, cut into 8 wedges

1 Heat oven to 425°. Spray jelly roll pan, 15 1/2 × 10 1/2 × 1 inch, with cooking spray. Mix parsley, marjoram, thyme, garlic salt and pepper. Spray both sides of pork chops with cooking spray. Sprinkle with 1 to 1 1/2 teaspoons herb mixture. Place in corners of pan.

2 Mix potatoes, mushrooms, bell pepper and onion in large bowl. Spray vegetables 2 or 3 times with cooking spray; stir. Sprinkle with remaining herb mixture; toss to coat. Spread evenly in center of pan between pork chops.

3 Bake uncovered 45 minutes. Turn pork; stir vegetables. Place tomato wedges over vegetables. Bake uncovered 10 to 15 minutes or until pork is slightly pink when cut near bone and vegetables are tender.

"This is a lot of food. It's as much as I need to keep going for a few hours, especially if I drink a glass of milk and eat whole wheat bread with it to get to my 4 choices."
                                                                                    —LORI S.

2
Carbohydrate
Choices

Speedy Pork Dinner

4 servings

**4 pork loin or rib chops
(1 to 1 1/4 pounds)**

1/4 cup beef or chicken broth

**4 medium potatoes,
cut into fourths**

**4 small carrots,
cut into 1-inch pieces**

**4 medium onions,
cut into fourths**

3/4 teaspoon salt

1/4 teaspoon pepper

**Chopped fresh parsley,
if desired**

PREP: **10 min**

COOK: **40 min**

1 Spray 12-inch nonstick skillet with cooking spray; heat over medium-high heat. Cook pork in skillet about 5 minutes, turning once, until brown.

2 Add broth, potatoes, carrots and onions to skillet. Sprinkle with salt and pepper. Heat to boiling; reduce heat. Cover and simmer about 30 minutes or until vegetables are tender and pork is slightly pink when cut near bone. Sprinkle with parsley.

note from **DR. B**
Not only do the potatoes, carrots and onions in this recipe fill you up, they add important nutrients such as fiber, vitamin A and vitamin C. Eating a variety of foods, such as meat and vegetables together, provides many nutrients to give your body all the benefits it requires.

1 SERVING: Calories 305

Fiber 5g	Sodium 570mg
Fat 8g (Saturated 3g)	Protein 27g
Cholesterol 65mg	Carbohydrate 36g

Food Exchanges: 1 1/2 Starch; 3 Very Lean Meat; 1 Vegetable

"Whenever a recipe calls for sour cream, I substitute plain yogurt. It's a healthy alternative and comes in a handy 32-ounce size convenient for cooking and baking."

—KATE D.

PREP: **15 min**

BAKE: **40 min**

Southwestern Pork Salad

4 servings

note from **DR. B**

The combination of pork, vegetables and peas in this recipe has created a very nutrient-dense, carbohydrate-controlled main-dish salad. That means for the calories it contains, it provides heaping amounts of protein, vitamins A and C, calcium, iron and fiber!

3/4 pound pork tenderloin

1/4 teaspoon salt

1/4 teaspoon pepper

Creamy Lime Dressing (below)

8 cups bite-size pieces mixed salad greens or 1 package (4 ounces) mixed salad greens

1 medium yellow bell pepper, sliced

1/2 pound mushrooms, sliced (3 cups)

1 can (15 to 16 ounces) black-eyed peas, rinsed and drained

1 Heat oven to 350°. Place pork on rack in shallow roasting pan. Sprinkle with salt and pepper. Insert meat thermometer so tip is in thickest part of pork.

2 Bake uncovered 30 to 40 minutes or until thermometer reads 160° (medium doneness) and pork is slightly pink in center. Meanwhile, make Creamy Lime Dressing. Cool pork; cut into slices.

3 Arrange salad greens, bell pepper, mushrooms and peas on large serving plate. Top with pork. Serve with dressing.

Creamy Lime Dressing

1/2 cup fat-free sour cream or plain yogurt

1/4 cup chopped fresh cilantro

2 tablespoons lime juice

2 tablespoons canola or vegetable oil

1/4 teaspoon salt

Mix all ingredients.

1 SERVING: Calories 325

Fiber 10g	Sodium 610mg
Fat 11g (Saturated 2g)	Protein 33g
Cholesterol 55mg	Carbohydrate 33g

Food Exchanges: 1 Starch; 4 Lean Meat; 1 Vegetable

Southwestern Pork Salad

"I was surprised to see a 'breaded' recipe at only 1/2 Carb Choice. I usually think of breading as being heavy, but this recipe fits easily into my eating plan."

—PAT A.

PREP: **10 min**
COOK: **10 min**

Breaded Pork Chops

8 servings

Betty's **success tip**

Breading fish, chicken, meat or vegetables doesn't have to be heavy. This one combines Bisquick, crackers and seasonings for a flavorful, low-carbohydrate option. Serve it with Rosemary-Parmesan Mashers (page 194) and Harvest Roasted Vegetables (page 198). Dessert's still a good possibility, if you have an additional Carbohydrate Choice in your meal plan.

1/2 cup Original Bisquick

12 saltine crackers, crushed (1/2 cup)

1 teaspoon seasoned salt

1/4 teaspoon pepper

1 egg or 1/4 cup fat-free cholesterol-free egg product

2 tablespoons water

8 pork boneless loin chops, 1/2 inch thick (about 2 pounds)

1 Mix Bisquick, cracker crumbs, seasoned salt and pepper. Mix egg and water.

2 Dip pork into egg mixture, then coat with Bisquick mixture.

3 Spray 12-inch nonstick skillet with cooking spray; heat over medium-high heat. Cook pork in skillet 8 to 10 minutes, turning once, until slightly pink in center.

1 SERVING: Calories 215

Fiber 0g	Sodium 370mg
Fat 10g (Saturated 3g)	Protein 24g
Cholesterol 90mg	Carbohydrate 8g

Food Exchanges: 1/2 Starch; 3 Lean Meat

"A sauce like this really helps control my sweet tooth. And it's a great way to make sure I get the fruit I need."
— *Tim H.*

PREP: **10 min**

COOK: **11 min**

Pan-Fried Ham with Sweet Balsamic-Peach Sauce

note from **DR. B**
A test called hemo-globin A1c provides a two- to three-month average of all your daily blood glucose readings. If you're not getting this done two to four times per year, ask your doctor to order this test. (See Diabetes Care Schedule, page 26.)

4 servings

1 pound fully cooked ham

1 bag (1 pound) frozen sliced peaches, thawed and drained

1/4 cup raspberry spreadable fruit

2 tablespoons packed brown sugar

1 tablespoon balsamic vinegar

1/4 teaspoon crushed red pepper, if desired

1 Cut ham into 4 slices, each about 1/4 inch thick.

2 Spray 12-inch nonstick skillet with cooking spray; heat over medium-high. Heat remaining ingredients in skillet about 6 minutes, stirring frequently, until peaches are tender and sauce is reduced to a glaze.

3 Add ham; reduce heat to medium. Cover and cook about 5 minutes, turning once, until ham is hot.

1 SERVING: Calories 230

Fiber 3g	Sodium 890mg
Fat 4g (Saturated 1g)	Protein 19g
Cholesterol 50mg	Carbohydrate 34g

Food Exchanges: 3 Very Lean Meat; 2 Fruit; 1 Fat

Chapter **5**

Great Grains, Legumes and Pasta

Grains, legumes and pasta are loaded with nutrients and fit beautifully into a diabetes meal plan. Enjoying meatless meals once a week can be a tasty way to include more whole grains, fiber, and other nutrients.

1-1½
Carbohydrate Choices

Barley and Asparagus 138

Bulgur Pilaf 137

Cheese Grits 140

———— 1½ ————

Cheesy Lentil and Green Bean Casserole 142

Fiesta Taco Salad with Beans 154

Potato-Tomato-Tofu Dinner 166

Savory Black-Eyed Peas 156

Wild Rice Salad with Dried Cherries 148

2
Carbohydrate Choices

Angel Hair with Avocado and Tomatoes 157

Creamy Quinoa Primavera 144

Fettuccine with Asparagus and Mushrooms 160

Garbanzo Bean Sandwiches 153

Orzo Parmesan 164

Ravioli with Tomato-Alfredo Sauce 159

Risotto Primavera 146

2½
Carbohydrate Choices

Countryside Pasta Toss 158

Five-Spice Tofu Stir-Fry 165

Harvest Salad 136

Rice Noodles with Peanut Sauce 162

Thai Vegetable Pizza 152

White Bean and Spinach Pizza 150

3
Carbohydrate Choices

Tropical Fruit, Rice and Tuna Salad 147

Vermicelli and Herbs 163

"I use my blood glucose monitor 1 1/2 hours after eating to see how my body reacts to certain foods. If my readings are high, next time I know to stay away from that food or to eat less of it."

—PAT A.

PREP: **20 min**

COOK: **20 min**

Harvest Salad

8 servings

1 cup uncooked quick-cooking barley

2 cups frozen whole kernel corn, thawed

1/2 cup dried cranberries

4 medium green onions, thinly sliced (1/4 cup)

1 medium unpeeled apple, chopped (1 cup)

1 small carrot, coarsely shredded (1/3 cup)

2 tablespoons canola or vegetable oil

2 tablespoons honey

1 tablespoon lemon juice

1 Cook barley in water as directed on package, omitting salt.

2 Mix barley, corn, cranberries, onions, apple and carrot in large bowl. Shake oil, honey and lemon juice in tightly covered container; pour over barley mixture and toss.

Betty's **success tip**

Quick-cooking barley contains all the nutrients of regular barley in a convenient, time-saving form. Combining grains, fruits and vegetables makes an interesting and good-for-you salad, one that's colorful and fancy enough to serve to company, but easy enough to make just for yourself and your family.

1 SERVING: Calories 195

Fiber 6g	Sodium 10mg
Fat 4g (Saturated 1g)	Protein 4g
Cholesterol 0mg	Carbohydrate 42g

Food Exchanges: 2 Starch; 1/2 Fruit

PREP: **15 min**

COOK: **25 min**

Bulgur Pilaf

6 servings

2 tablespoons canola oil or butter, melted

1/2 cup slivered almonds

1 medium onion, chopped (1/2 cup)

1 medium carrot, chopped (1/2 cup)

1 can (14 ounces) chicken broth

1 cup uncooked bulgur

1/4 teaspoon lemon pepper seasoning salt or black pepper

1/4 cup chopped fresh parsley

1 Heat 1 tablespoon of the oil in 12-inch skillet over medium-high heat. Cook almonds in oil 2 to 3 minutes, stirring constantly, until golden brown. Remove almonds from skillet.

2 Add remaining 1 tablespoon oil, the onion and carrot to skillet. Cook about 3 minutes, stirring occasionally, until vegetables are crisp-tender.

3 Stir in broth, bulgur and lemon pepper seasoning salt. Heat to boiling; reduce heat. Cover and simmer about 15 minutes or until bulgur is tender and liquid is absorbed. Stir in almonds and parsley.

note from **DR. B**

Bulgur is made from wheat berries that have been partially cooked and cracked. Bulgur, a whole-grain, imparts a nutty, whole wheat flavor with plenty of nutrients, such as phosphorus and iron.

1 SERVING: Calories 140

Fiber 4g	Sodium 630mg
Fat 9g (Saturated 3g)	Protein 5g
Cholesterol 10mg	Carbohydrate 13g

Food Exchanges: 1 Starch; 1 1/2 Fat

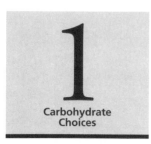

1

Carbohydrate
Choices

Betty's **success tip**

Cooking grains in chicken, beef or vegetable broth adds to the overall flavor of the dish. You can also cook grains like barley, rice, quinoa or bulgur in apple juice or eight-vegetable juice for extra flavor.

"I'm always trying to eat more grains and vegetables, and I love trying them combined. In this recipe, I could use a reduced-sodium and low-fat, or even fat-free, version of the chicken broth."
—LORI S.

Barley and Asparagus

8 servings

2 tablespoons canola oil or butter

1 medium onion, chopped (1/2 cup)

1 medium carrot, chopped (1/2 cup)

1 cup uncooked quick-cooking barley

2 cans (14 ounces each) chicken broth, heated

8 ounces asparagus (8 to 10 stalks), cut into 1-inch pieces

2 tablespoons shredded Parmesan cheese

1/4 teaspoon dried marjoram or thyme leaves

1/8 teaspoon pepper

1 Heat oil in 12-inch skillet over medium heat. Cook onion and carrot in oil 1 to 2 minutes, stirring occasionally, until crisp-tender. Stir in barley. Cook and stir 1 minute.

2 Pour 1 cup of the hot broth over barley mixture. Cook uncovered about 5 minutes, stirring occasionally, until liquid is absorbed. Stir in asparagus. Continue cooking 15 to 20 minutes, adding broth 1 cup at a time and stirring frequently, until barley is tender and liquid is absorbed; remove from heat. Stir in remaining ingredients.

1 SERVING: (ABOUT 1/2 CUP):
Calories 130

Fiber 5g	Sodium 520mg
Fat 4g (Saturated 2g)	Protein 6g
Cholesterol 10mg	Carbohydrate 23g

Food Exchanges: 1 Starch; 1 Vegetable; 1/2 Fat

Barley and Asparagus and Parmesan-Dijon Chicken (page 78)

PREP: **20 min**

BAKE: **40 min**

STAND: **10 min**

note from **DR. B**

Matching the amount of food you eat with the amount of medication you take will help you avoid high and low blood glucose values. If you'd like to make this recipe your main dish, just double your serving to equal 2 Carbohydrate Choices, and enjoy with a fresh vegetable or salad.

"I started a walking club in my neighborhood because so many of us like to walk. It's much more fun when there are a few of us together. Sometimes we make our last stop at a member's house and enjoy a tasty, low-fat snack or a glass of ice water with a fresh lemon twist."

—PAT A.

Cheese Grits

8 servings

2 cups fat-free (skim) milk

2 cups water

1/2 teaspoon salt

1/4 teaspoon pepper

1 cup uncooked white hominy quick grits

1 1/2 cups shredded Cheddar cheese (6 ounces)

2 medium green onions, sliced (2 tablespoons)

2 eggs, slightly beaten or 1/2 cup fat-free cholesterol-free egg product

1 tablespoon butter or margarine, cut into small pieces

1/4 teaspoon paprika

1 Heat oven to 350°. Grease bottom and side of 1 1/2-quart casserole with shortening or spray with cooking spray.

2 Heat milk, water, salt and pepper to boiling in 2-quart saucepan. Gradually add grits, stirring constantly; reduce heat. Simmer uncovered about 5 minutes, stirring frequently, until thickened. Stir in cheese and onions.

3 Stir 1 cup of the grits mixture into eggs, then stir back into remaining grits in saucepan. Pour into casserole. Sprinkle butter and paprika over grits.

4 Bake uncovered 35 to 40 minutes or until set. Let stand 10 minutes before serving.

1 SERVING: Calories 235

Fiber 0g

Fat 11g
(Saturated 7g)

Cholesterol 85mg

Sodium 360mg

Protein 12g

Carbohydrate 19g

Food Exchanges: 1 Starch; 1 Medium-Fat Meat; 1 1/2 Fat

What's So Great About Whole Grains?

How can whole grains help diabetes? Eating whole-grain foods gives you fiber, vitamins, minerals and hundreds of phytonutrients (health-protective substances found in plant foods) that work together in powerful ways to help protect against heart disease and certain cancers.

Q. **What are whole grains?**

A. Whole grains include all three parts of a grain: the bran, germ and endosperm. By eating all three parts, you get the entire package of nutrients.

Q. **How do I know if a food is made from whole grains?**

A. Read the ingredient list on the package. The word "whole" or "whole grain" before the grain's name tells you that a food is made from the entire grain. Wheat, corn, oats and rice are the most common varieties of grains eaten in the United States. You'll find them in cereals, breads, crackers and pasta. Look for foods that include a statement on the package, called a health claim, or a whole-grain seal to ensure that you're getting a whole-grain product.

Q. **How can I cook with whole grains—don't they take a long time to prepare?**

A. Some whole grains, like wheat berries, brown rice and barley take a long time to cook. However, if you have the time, it's worth the extra effort because they're delicious *and* good for you. Whole grains such as quinoa, bulgur wheat, quick-cooking barley and oatmeal cook quickly. Baking with like old-fashioned oatmeal adds flavor, texture and nutrients to your baked goods.

Go with the Grain

"Three are key" can help you remember to eat three whole grains (or more) every day. To get your grains:

- *Eat whole-grain cereal* or granola bars for breakfast or as a snack.

- *Choose whole-grain breads* for toast and sandwiches. Breads with 2 to 3 grams of fiber per serving are good choices.

- *Substitute old-fashioned oatmeal,* cooked bulgur or brown rice for the bread crumbs and one-third of the meat in meat loaves and meatballs.

- *Add raw or cooked barley* or brown rice to your favorite vegetable soup.

- *Cook extra whole grains,* then set aside half to make pilafs, toss in salads and use in soups or casseroles.

- *Bake breads or muffins* with oatmeal, whole-wheat flour and whole-grain cornmeal. Choose recipes that include whole grains, or experiment by replacing about one-third of the regular flour with whole-grain flour.

PREP: **5 min**
BAKE: **1 hr 30 min**

note from **DR. B**

To reduce fat, calories and cholesterol, eat meatless meals as often as you can; aim for one or two per week. Continue to count your carbohydrates— meatless meals often provide more carbo- hydrates than meat- based meals.

Cheesy Lentil and Green Bean Casserole

6 servings

1 cup dried lentils (8 ounces), sorted and rinsed

1/2 cup uncooked brown rice

2 cans (14 ounces each) chicken broth

1/4 cup water

1/4 teaspoon salt

1 cup shredded reduced-fat Cheddar cheese (4 ounces)

1 bag (1 pound) frozen cut green beans or broccoli cuts, thawed and drained

1 Heat oven to 375°. Mix lentils, rice, broth, water, salt and 3/4 cup of the cheese in 2-quart casserole. Cover and bake 1 hour.

2 Stir in green beans. Cover and bake about 30 minutes or until liquid is absorbed and rice is tender. Sprinkle with remaining 1/4 cup cheese.

1 SERVING: Calories 200

Fiber 10g	Sodium 840mg
Fat 3g	
(Saturated 1g)	Protein 18g
Cholesterol 5mg	Carbohydrate 35g

Food Exchanges: 1 1/2 Starch; 1 1/2 Very Lean Meat; 1 Vegetable

Less Fat, Not Flavor

If you're trying to lose weight, control cholesterol or lower your blood pressure, it's important to cut back on the total amount of fat you consume. But don't try to deprive yourself too much or you'll find it hard to stick to your eating plan. Getting started can be the hardest part. These simple suggestions can help you begin:

- *Pay attention to portion size* and eat less. As portions grow, so do calories and fat. Skip the super-size meals and snacks, and choose normal-size servings. Load up on vegetables if you're still hungry.

- *Trim visible fat* from meat and poultry. If you cook chicken or turkey with the skin on, remove it before eating.

- *Choose reduced-fat* mayonnaise, salad dressings and sour cream.

- *Go light on added fat* like butter, margarine and cream sauces. Use half as much as you are used to, or eliminate them when you can.

- *Cut back on high-fat snacks,* like chips, French fries, high-fat cheeses and baked goods like doughnuts, muffins and cookies.

Monounsaturated Fat

Monounsaturated (good) fat, found mostly in plant foods, is a better choice than saturated fat. It's easy to add more to your diet by:

- **Using canola or olive oil when cooking, sautéing and baking**

- **Adding nuts to stir-fries, salads, snacks and desserts**

- **Incorporating small amounts of avocados and olives into your diet by topping salads and casseroles**

- *Cook lean* whenever possible. Broil, bake, roast, grill, poach, steam, stew or microwave when you're cooking at home or ordering at a restaurant.

- *Select lean skinless cuts* of chicken and turkey or lean meat. The leanest pork cuts are tenderloin and loin chop. The leanest beef cuts are tenderloin, top round or eye of round.

- *Go meatless at least twice* each week. Limiting the amount of meat you eat can help reduce fat, particularly saturated fat. Instead of meat, try dried beans and peas, grains, vegetables and fruits, which increase fiber and complex carbohydrates.

- *Use low-fat or fat-free dairy products* such as reduced-fat and fat-free yogurt, cheese, pudding, milk and ice cream. Dairy products made from whole milk or cream have extra calories along with the extra fat.

- *Eat fish once or twice* each week. Higher-fat fish such as tuna and salmon contain omega-3 fatty acids, the kind of fat that can help your heart!

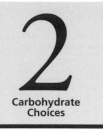

2

Carbohydrate
Choices

PREP: **5 min**

COOK: **22 min**

note from **DR. B**

Regular, consistent exercise helps your body use insulin more effectively, all day and night. Physical activity also reduces the risk of heart attacks. Aim for a total of 30 to 60 minutes of moderate activity on most days. To reduce the risk of hypoglycemia (low blood glucose), exercise at the same time of day, each day.

"Diet and medicine are only part of the treatment of diabetes—exercise is a huge part that's easy to skip when my schedule gets hectic! I really have to push myself, but I always feel better after exercising and my blood sugars are great."

—KATE D.

Creamy Quinoa Primavera

6 servings

1 1/2 cups uncooked quinoa

3 cups chicken broth

1 package (3 ounces) cream cheese

1 tablespoon chopped fresh or 1 teaspoon dried basil leaves

2 teaspoons canola oil or butter

2 cloves garlic, finely chopped

5 cups thinly sliced or bite-size pieces assorted vegetables (such as asparagus, broccoli, carrot, zucchini)

2 tablespoons grated Romano cheese

1 Rinse quinoa thoroughly; drain. Heat quinoa and broth to boiling in 2-quart saucepan; reduce heat. Cover and simmer 10 to 15 minutes or until all broth is absorbed. Stir in cream cheese and basil.

2 Heat oil in 10-inch nonstick skillet over medium-high heat. Cook garlic in oil about 30 seconds, stirring frequently, until golden. Stir in vegetables. Cook about 5 minutes, stirring frequently, until vegetables are crisp-tender. Toss vegetables and quinoa mixture. Sprinkle with Romano cheese.

1 SERVING: Calories 260

Fiber 5g	Sodium 630mg
Fat 10g (Saturated 5g)	Protein 12g
Cholesterol 80mg	Carbohydrate 36g

Food Exchanges: 2 Starch; 1/2 Medium-Fat Meat; 1 Vegetable; 1 Fat

Creamy Quinoa Primavera

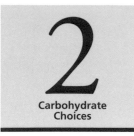

2

Carbohydrate
Choices

"My dietitian suggested keeping a journal of the foods I eat and the blood glucose readings I get. That way, I can track what makes my glucose shoot up and what keeps it more stable. At first it was hard to remember, but now I'm used to it and even enjoy it!"

—PAT A.

PREP: **15 min**

COOK: **20 min**

Risotto Primavera

7 servings

Betty's **success tip**

Traditional risotto often includes high-fat dairy products such as butter, half-and-half and cream. This lower-fat version relies on the sweetness of carrots and other vegetables as well as Parmesan cheese to give it extra flavor.

1 tablespoon olive or canola oil

1 medium onion, chopped (1/2 cup)

1 small carrot, cut into julienne strips (1/2 cup)

1 cup uncooked Arborio or other short-grain rice

2 cans (14 ounces each) chicken broth

1 cup broccoli flowerets

1 cup frozen green peas

1 small zucchini, cut into julienne strips (1/2 cup)

1/4 cup grated Parmesan cheese

1 Heat oil in 3-quart nonstick saucepan over medium-high heat. Cook onion and carrot in oil, stirring frequently, until crisp-tender. Stir in rice. Cook, stirring frequently, until rice begins to brown.

2 Pour 1/2 cup of the broth over rice mixture. Cook uncovered, stirring occasionally, until liquid is absorbed. Continue cooking 15 to 20 minutes, adding broth 1/2 cup at a time and stirring occasionally, until rice is tender and creamy; add broccoli, peas and zucchini with the last addition of broth. Sprinkle with cheese.

1 SERVING: Calories 175

Fiber 2g	Sodium 640mg
Fat 4g (Saturated 1g);	Protein 8g
Cholesterol 5mg	Carbohydrate 29g

Food Exchanges: 1 1/2 Starch; 1 Vegetable; 1/2 Fat

"This is a healthier version of an old recipe I used to make. My kids like the fact that there's fruit in the salad—so it has a sweeter taste." —BETTY H.

Tropical Fruit, Rice and Tuna Salad

4 servings

PREP: **20 min**
CHILL: **2 hr**

1 1/2 cups cold cooked brown or white rice

1/2 cup vanilla artificially sweetened low-fat yogurt

1 can (8 ounces) pineapple tidbits in juice, drained and 1 teaspoon juice reserved

2 kiwifruit, peeled and sliced

1 medium mango, peeled and chopped (1 cup)

1 can (6 ounces) albacore tuna in water, drained and flaked

1 tablespoon coconut, toasted (page 212)

1 Mix rice, yogurt and 1 teaspoon reserved pineapple juice in medium bowl. Cover and refrigerate 1 to 2 hours to blend flavors.

2 Cut kiwifruit slices into fourths. Gently stir kiwifruit, pineapple, mango and tuna into rice mixture. Sprinkle with coconut.

Betty's success tip

When you're cooking rice, why not cook an extra batch? You can cover and refrigerate it up to 5 days or freeze it up to 4 months. Then you'll be ready at a moment's notice for recipes like this one that use already cooked rice.

1 SERVING: Calories 225

Fiber 4g	Sodium 170mg
Fat 2g (Saturated 1g)	Protein 15g
Cholesterol 15mg	Carbohydrate 41g

Food Exchanges: 2 Starch; 1 Very Lean Meat; 1/2 Fruit

"There's always lots of food around where I work. One thing that helps me is to make sure that I eat a hearty breakfast and lunch. That way, I'm not quite as tempted to indulge in oversized cookies and other high-sugar-containing foods."

—KATE D.

PREP: **20 min**

COOK: **20 min**

note from **DR. B**

Peanuts contain the same compound found in red wine that scientists believe may lower blood cholesterol levels. Peanuts are also rich in monounsaturated fat, vitamin E and folic acid, all heart-healthy nutrients. Include some in your diet, but control the amount you eat because the calories do add up.

Wild Rice Salad with Dried Cherries

7 servings

1 package (6.2 ounces) fast-cooking long-grain and wild rice mix

1 medium unpeeled eating apple, chopped (1 cup)

1 medium green bell pepper, chopped (1 cup)

1 medium stalk celery, chopped (1/2 cup)

1/2 cup dried cherries, chopped

2 tablespoons soy sauce

2 tablespoons water

2 teaspoons sugar

2 teaspoons cider vinegar

1/3 cup dry-roasted peanuts, toasted (page 50)

1 Cook rice mix as directed on package—except omit butter. Spread rice evenly in thin layer on large ungreased cookie sheet. Let stand 10 to 12 minutes, stirring occasionally, until cool.

2 Mix apple, bell pepper, celery and cherries in large bowl. Mix soy sauce, water, sugar and vinegar in small bowl until sugar is dissolved. Add rice and soy sauce mixture to apple mixture. Gently toss until coated. Add peanuts; gently toss.

1 SERVING: Calories 125

Fiber 2g	Sodium 300mg
Fat 4g (Saturated 1g)	Protein 3g
Cholesterol 0mg	Carbohydrate 21g

Food Exchanges: 1 Starch; 1/2 Fruit

Wild Rice Salad with Dried Cherries

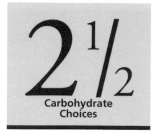
"I just love pizza and didn't want to give it up, but it really made my blood sugars shoot up. Now I order thin crust and make sure I eat other foods with it. This recipe is a tasty alternative to higher-fat and -calorie pizza."

—SAMMY E.

PREP: **15 min**

BAKE: **10 min**

White Bean and Spinach Pizza

6 servings

Betty's **success tip**

When picking out your pizza crust, think thin. The thick-crust variety is much higher in carbohydrates, calories and fat per serving.

1/2 cup sun-dried tomato halves (not in oil)

1 can (15 to 16 ounces) great northern or navy beans, rinsed and drained

2 medium cloves garlic, finely chopped

1 package (10 ounces) ready-to-serve thin Italian pizza crust (12 inches in diameter)

1/4 teaspoon dried oregano leaves

1 cup firmly packed spinach leaves, shredded

1/2 cup shredded reduced-fat Colby-Monterey Jack cheese (2 ounces)

1 Heat oven to 425°. Pour enough boiling water over dried tomatoes to cover. Let stand 10 minutes; drain. Cut into thin strips; set aside.

2 Place beans and garlic in food processor. Cover and process until smooth.

3 Spread beans over pizza crust. Sprinkle with oregano, tomatoes, spinach and cheese. Place on ungreased cookie sheet. Bake about 10 minutes or until cheese is melted.

1 SERVING: Calories 233

Fiber 6g	Sodium 550mg
Fat 2g (Saturated 1g)	Protein 15g
Cholesterol 50mg	Carbohydrate 46g

Food Exchanges: 2 Starch; 1 Very Lean Meat; 2 Vegetable

White Bean and Spinach Pizza

PREP: **9 min**

BAKE: **20 min**

Thai Vegetable Pizza

6 servings

6 flour tortillas (8 to 10 inches in diameter)

6 tablespoons peanut butter

1/4 cup soy sauce

2 tablespoons seasoned rice vinegar

2 teaspoons sugar

1 cup shredded mozzarella cheese (4 ounces)

2 cups fresh bean sprouts

1 bag (1 pound) frozen stir-fry vegetables, thawed and drained

1 Heat oven to 400°. Place tortillas on ungreased cookie sheet. Bake 5 minutes.

2 Mix peanut butter, soy sauce, vinegar and sugar; spread over tortillas. Top each with 2 tablespoons cheese. Spread bean sprouts and stir-fry vegetables evenly over tortillas. Sprinkle with remaining cheese.

3 Bake 10 to 15 minutes or until cheese is melted.

1 SERVING: Calories 345

Fiber 5g	Sodium 960mg
Fat 15g (Saturated 4g)	Protein 19g
Cholesterol 10mg	Carbohydrate 38g

Food Exchanges: 2 Starch; 2 Medium-Fat Meat; 1 Vegetable

"To make good food choices, I've gotten used to carrying my lunch. In fact, people kid me that I bring my food with me wherever I go. It's pretty easy to make this filling at home and bring it along with the bread and dressing for a great lunch at work."
—BILL A.

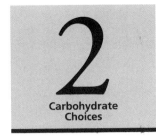

Garbanzo Bean Sandwiches

PREP: **15 min**

6 servings

1 can (15 to 16 ounces) garbanzo beans, rinsed and drained

1/2 cup water

2 tablespoons chopped fresh parsley

2 tablespoons chopped walnuts

1 tablespoon chopped onion

1 clove garlic, chopped

1/2 medium cucumber, sliced

4 whole wheat pita breads (6 inches in diameter)

Lettuce leaves

1 medium tomato, seeded and chopped (3/4 cup)

1/2 cup cucumber ranch dressing

1 Place beans, water, parsley, walnuts, onion and garlic in food processor or blender. Cover and process until smooth.

2 Cut cucumber into slices. Cut each pita bread in half to form 2 pockets; line with lettuce leaves. Spoon 2 tablespoons bean spread into each pita half. Add tomato, cucumber and dressing.

Betty's **success tip**

Nuts and seeds are great little nuggets of nutrients, but adding them in moderation is best because they can be high in fat. Fortunately, a little goes a long way in terms of flavor, and when nuts and seeds are lightly toasted, they become flavor giants!

1 SERVING (1 1/2 SANDWICHES):
Calories 295

Fiber 8g	Sodium 590mg
Fat 13g (Saturated 1g)	Protein 11g
Cholesterol 5mg	Carbohydrate 40g

Food Exchanges: 1/2 Lean Meat; 2 Starch; 1 1/2 Fat

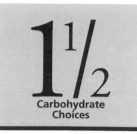

1 1/2
Carbohydrate Choices

PREP: **15 min**

COOK: **3 min**

note from **DR. B**

This nutrient-dense recipe is a powerhouse! That means for the amount of calories it provides, it's loaded with vitamins and minerals including fiber, calcium, iron, magnesium and vitamin C. Individuals with diabetes tend to lose more magnesium than other people do, which can lead to muscle cramps.

Fiesta Taco Salad with Beans

5 servings

1 can (15 ounces) black beans, rinsed and drained

1/2 cup taco sauce

6 cups bite-size pieces lettuce

1 medium green bell pepper, cut into strips

2 medium tomatoes, cut into wedges

1/2 cup pitted ripe olives, drained

1 cup corn chips

1 cup shredded Cheddar cheese (4 ounces)

1/2 cup reduced-fat Thousand Island dressing

1 Heat beans and taco sauce in 2-quart saucepan over medium heat 2 to 3 minutes, stirring occasionally, until heated.

2 Toss lettuce, bell pepper, tomatoes, olives and corn chips in large bowl. Spoon bean mixture over lettuce mixture; toss. Sprinkle with cheese. Serve immediately with dressing.

1 SERVING: Calories 270

Fiber 8g

Fat 12g
(Saturated 5g)

Cholesterol 25mg

Sodium 730mg

Protein 18g

Carbohydrate 31g

Food Exchanges: 1 1/2 Starch; 2 Medium-Fat Meat

Fiesta Taco Salad with Beans

PREP: **20 min**

COOK: **53 min**

Savory Black-Eyed Peas

4 servings

note from **DR. B**

The black-eyed peas and cheese provide plenty of fiber, protein, calcium and iron, and combining them with the vegetables gives you the goodness of vitamins A and C. It's an excellent dish for a weeknight meatless meal.

2 1/2 cups chicken broth

1 cup dried black-eyed peas
(8 ounces), sorted and rinsed

2 medium stalks celery, sliced
(1 cup)

1 large onion, chopped
(1 cup)

1 1/2 tablespoons chopped
fresh or 1 1/2 teaspoons
dried savory leaves

1 clove garlic, finely chopped

3 medium carrots,
thinly sliced (1 1/2 cups)

1 large green bell pepper,
cut into 1-inch pieces

1/2 cup shredded Monterey
Jack cheese with jalapeño
peppers (2 ounces)

1 Heat broth, black-eyed peas, celery, onion, savory and garlic to boiling in 10-inch skillet. Boil uncovered 2 minutes; reduce heat. Cover and simmer about 40 minutes, stirring occasionally, until peas are almost tender (do not boil or peas will fall apart).

2 Stir in carrots and bell pepper. Heat to simmering. Cover and simmer about 13 minutes, stirring occasionally, until vegetables are tender; stir. Sprinkle with cheese.

1 SERVING: Calories 255

Fiber 11g	Sodium 870mg
Fat 9g (Saturated 4g)	Protein 19g
Cholesterol 20mg	Carbohydrate 36g

Food Exchanges: 1 Starch;
1 1/2 Medium-Fat Meat;
2 Vegetable

"Whenever I cook pasta for six, I always measure out one-sixth of the pasta and one-sixth of the sauce for my portion first. Then I toss the rest for the others eating with me. Otherwise it's very difficult to get the right-sized portion."

—PAT A.

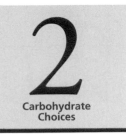

2

Carbohydrate
Choices

PREP: **15 min**

COOK: **5 min**

Angel Hair with Avocado and Tomatoes

6 servings

8 ounces uncooked capellini (angel hair) pasta

2 tablespoons olive or canola oil

2 cloves garlic, finely chopped

3/4 cup chopped fresh basil leaves

1 small avocado, peeled, pitted and cut into small cubes

4 medium tomatoes, cut into small cubes

1/2 teaspoon salt

1/4 teaspoon pepper

1 Cook and drain pasta as directed on package.

2 While pasta is cooking, heat oil in 3-quart saucepan over medium heat. Cook garlic in oil about 5 minutes, stirring occasionally, until garlic is tender but not brown; remove from heat.

3 Stir basil, avocado and tomatoes into garlic in saucepan. Toss vegetable mixture and pasta. Sprinkle with salt and pepper.

note from **DR. B**

Even if you are taking a diabetes medica-tion, following your food plan will improve your blood glucose control. If you don't have a food plan, make an appointment to see a diabetes nutrition specialist or dietitian trained to be a Certified Diabetes Educator. (See Tap into Resources, page 27.)

1 SERVING: Calories 220

Fiber 3g	Sodium 210mg
Fat 10g (Saturated 1g)	Protein 6g
Cholesterol 30mg	Carbohydrate 30g

Food Exchanges: 1 1/2 Starch; 1 Vegetable; 2 Fat

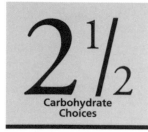

2 1/2
Carbohydrate
Choices

PREP: **10 min**
COOK: **10 min**

"I've been using the new whole wheat pasta, and I really like it. It comes in lots of great shapes!"
—LORI S.

Countryside Pasta Toss

4 servings

1 cup uncooked rotini pasta
(3 ounces)

3/4 pound new potatoes,
cut into 1/2-inch wedges

1 cup baby-cut carrots

1 cup broccoli flowerets

1/2 cup snap pea pods

1 tablespoon butter or
margarine

2 tablespoons chopped
fresh parsley

1 teaspoon dried dill weed

1/2 teaspoon salt

4 ounces fully cooked ham,
cut into thin strips

1 Cook and drain pasta as directed on package.

2 While pasta is cooking, place steamer basket in 1/2 inch water in 3-quart saucepan (water should not touch bottom of basket). Place potatoes and carrots in basket. Cover tightly and heat to boiling; reduce heat to medium-low. Steam 5 minutes. Add broccoli and pea pods. Cover and steam about 2 minutes longer or until potatoes are tender.

3 Place vegetables in medium bowl. Add butter, parsley, dill weed and salt; toss. Add ham and pasta; toss.

1 SERVING: Calories 275

Fiber 5g

Fat 7g
(Saturated 2g)

Cholesterol
15mg

Sodium
760mg

Protein 13g

Carbohydrate
45g

Food Exchanges: 2 Starch;
2 Vegetable; 1 Medium-Fat Meat

"I know traditional Alfredo sauce is high in fat. What's great about this recipe is that it combines tomato and Alfredo. That means it's lower fat and it still tastes creamy and delicious!"

—Tim H.

Ravioli with Tomato-Alfredo Sauce

PREP: **10 min**
COOK: **10 min**

6 servings

2 packages (9 ounces each) refrigerated cheese-filled ravioli

1 package (8 ounces) sliced mushrooms (3 cups)

1 large onion, coarsely chopped (1 cup)

1 jar (24 to 28 ounces) tomato pasta sauce (any variety)

1/2 cup half-and-half, fat-free half-and-half or refrigerated fat-free nondairy creamer

1/4 cup grated Parmesan cheese

1/4 cup chopped fresh parsley

1 Cook and drain ravioli as directed on package; keep warm.

2 Spray 2-quart saucepan with cooking spray; heat over medium heat. Cook mushrooms and onion in saucepan about 5 minutes, stirring frequently, until onion is crisp-tender.

3 Stir in pasta sauce and half-and-half. Heat to boiling; reduce heat to low. Stir in ravioli, cheese and parsley. Sprinkle with additional cheese if desired.

note from **DR. B**
One of the most common reasons for giving up on exercise is doing too much too soon and burning out. If you set reasonable, achievable goals, you'll be more likely to stick with a program. When you reach your short-term goal, set another one. And don't forget to reward yourself!

1 SERVING: Calories 215

Fiber 2g	Sodium 1100mg
Fat 7g (Saturated 4g)	Protein 12g
Cholesterol 85mg	Carbohydrate 30g

Food Exchanges: 2 Starch; 1 Medium-Fat Meat

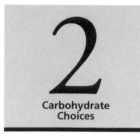

2

Carbohydrate Choices

PREP: **10 min**

COOK: **10 min**

note from **DR. B**

This pasta dish is a bit lower in protein, so serve it with a slice of whole wheat bread and cheese. Or serve as a side dish to meat. You need to get enough protein every day to help build new cells and make antibodies to fight off infection.

Fettuccine with Asparagus and Mushrooms

7 servings

1/4 cup sun-dried tomatoes (not in oil)

8 ounces uncooked fettuccine

1 teaspoon olive or canola oil

1 pound thin asparagus, broken into 2-inch pieces

1 pound mushrooms, sliced (6 cups)

2 cloves garlic, finely chopped

3 tablespoons chopped fresh parsley

2 tablespoons chopped fresh basil leaves

2 tablespoons cornstarch

1/2 teaspoon salt

1/4 teaspoon pepper

1 cup dry white wine or chicken broth

1 cup chicken broth

1/4 cup pine nuts

1/4 cup freshly grated Parmesan cheese

1 Pour enough boiling water over dried tomatoes to cover. Let stand 10 minutes; drain. Chop tomatoes.

2 Cook and drain fettuccine as directed on package.

3 While fettuccine is cooking, heat oil in 12-inch skillet over medium heat. Cook asparagus, mushrooms, garlic, parsley and basil in oil 5 minutes, stirring occasionally. Stir in tomatoes. Simmer 2 to 3 minutes or until tomatoes are heated.

4 Beat cornstarch, salt and pepper into wine and broth in small bowl with wire whisk; stir into vegetable mixture. Heat to boiling over medium heat, stirring constantly, until mixture is smooth and bubbly; boil and stir 1 minute. Serve over fettuccine. Sprinkle with nuts and cheese.

1 SERVING: Calories 210

Fiber 3g

Fat 7g

(Saturated 2g)

Cholesterol 30mg

Sodium 580mg

Protein 10g

Carbohydrate 30g

Food Exchanges: 1 Starch; 3 Vegetable; 1 Fat

Fettuccine with Asparagus and Mushrooms

PREP: **15 min**

Rice Noodles with Peanut Sauce

6 servings

8 ounces uncooked rice stick noodles

1/2 cup creamy peanut butter

2 tablespoons soy sauce

1 teaspoon grated gingerroot

1/2 teaspoon crushed red pepper

1/2 cup chicken broth or water

4 ounces canned bean sprouts

1 small red bell pepper, cut into 1/4-inch strips

2 medium green onions, sliced (2 tablespoons)

2 tablespoons chopped fresh cilantro, if desired

1 Heat 2 quarts water to boiling. Break noodles in half and pull apart slightly; drop into boiling water. Cook uncovered 1 minute; drain. Rinse with cold water; drain.

2 Mix peanut butter, soy sauce, gingerroot and red pepper in small bowl with wire whisk until smooth. Gradually mix in broth.

3 Place noodles in large bowl. Add peanut butter mixture, bean sprouts, bell pepper and onions; toss. Sprinkle with cilantro.

1 SERVING: Calories 305

Fiber 3g	Sodium 520mg
Fat 13g (Saturated 2g)	Protein 10g
Cholesterol 0mg	Carbohydrate 40g

Food Exchanges: 2 Starch; 2 Vegetable; 2 Fat

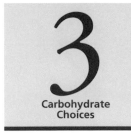

3

Carbohydrate
Choices

PREP: **10 min**

COOK: **9 min**

Vermicelli and Herbs

4 servings

8 ounces uncooked vermicelli

2 tablespoons olive or canola oil

2 tablespoons chopped pine nuts

1 tablespoon chopped fresh parsley

1 tablespoon large capers, chopped

1 teaspoon chopped fresh rosemary leaves

1 teaspoon chopped fresh sage leaves

1 teaspoon chopped fresh basil leaves

1 cup cherry tomatoes, cut into fourths

Freshly ground pepper, if desired

1 Cook and drain vermicelli as directed on package.

2 Mix remaining ingredients except tomatoes and pepper in medium bowl. Stir in tomatoes. Toss vermicelli and herb mixture. Sprinkle with pepper.

Betty's **success tip**

Herbs, especially fresh ones, impart an extra flavor boost to foods. To cut fat and calories, serve meatless meals at least once a week. For a great veggie side, select Corn- and Pepper-Stuffed Zucchini (page 202) or Mediterranean Vegetable Salad (page 207).

1 SERVING: Calories 290

Fiber 3g	Sodium 65mg
Fat 11g (Saturated 1g)	Protein 9g
Cholesterol 0mg	Carbohydrate 48g

Food Exchanges: 3 Starch; 2 Fat

2

Carbohydrate
Choices

PREP: **10 min**

COOK: **15 min**

"When I want a treat, I buy myself a piece of clothing or household item that I've had my eye on instead of treating myself with something to eat. Half the battle is won when you can change the way you think." —SHERRY L.

Orzo Parmesan

6 servings

1 can (14 ounces)
chicken broth

1/2 cup water

1/4 teaspoon salt

1 1/3 cups uncooked orzo
or rosamarina pasta

2 cloves garlic, finely
chopped

8 medium green onions,
sliced (1/2 cup)

1/3 cup grated Parmesan
cheese

1 tablespoon chopped
fresh or 1 teaspoon dried
basil leaves

1/8 teaspoon freshly
ground pepper

1 Heat broth, water and salt to boiling in 2-quart saucepan. Stir in pasta, garlic and onions. Heat to boiling; reduce heat. Cover and simmer about 12 minutes, stirring occasionally, until most of the liquid is absorbed.

2 Stir in remaining ingredients.

1 SERVING: Calories 145

Fiber 2g	Sodium 510mg
Fat 3g (Saturated 1g)	Protein 8g
Cholesterol 0mg	Carbohydrate 28g

Food Exchanges: 2 Starch; 1/2 Fat

Five-Spice Tofu Stir-Fry

2 1/2
Carbohydrate Choices

PREP: **15 min**
STAND: **10 min**
COOK: **18 min**

4 servings

1/4 cup stir-fry sauce

2 tablespoons orange juice

1 tablespoon honey

3/4 teaspoon five-spice powder

1 package (14 ounces) firm tofu, cut into 3/4-inch cubes

1 small red onion, cut into thin wedges

1 bag (1 pound) frozen baby beans and carrots (or other combination)

1/4 cup water

2 cups hot cooked rice

1 Mix stir-fry sauce, orange juice, honey and five-spice powder in medium bowl. Press tofu between paper towels to absorb excess moisture. Stir into sauce mixture. Let stand 10 minutes to marinate.

2 Spray 12-inch nonstick skillet with cooking spray; heat over medium heat. Remove tofu from sauce mixture; reserve sauce mixture. Cook tofu in skillet 3 to 4 minutes, stirring occasionally, just until light golden brown; remove from skillet.

3 Add onion to skillet. Cook 2 minutes, stirring occasionally. Add frozen vegetables and water. Heat to boiling; reduce heat to medium. Cover and cook 6 to 8 minutes, stirring occasionally, until vegetables are crisp-tender.

4 Stir in reserved sauce mixture and tofu. Cook 2 to 3 minutes, stirring occasionally, until mixture is slightly thickened and hot. Serve over rice.

note *from* **DR. B**

Soy foods, such as tofu and roasted soy nuts, contain complex carbohydrates, protein and heart-healthy fat. Research is being conducted to find out whether soybeans may actually help prevent or delay the development of type 2 diabetes and heart disease.

1 SERVING: Calories 295

Fiber 5g	Sodium 750mg
Fat 7g (Saturated 1g)	Protein 18g
Cholesterol 0mg	Carbohydrate 45g

Food Exchanges: 2 1/2 Starch; 1 1/2 Lean Meat

PREP: **10 min**
COOK: **21 min**

Potato-Tomato-Tofu Dinner

4 servings

2 tablespoons olive or canola oil

1/2 cup coarsely chopped red onion

5 small red potatoes, sliced (2 1/2 cups)

2 cups frozen cut green beans

1/2 teaspoon Italian seasoning

1/2 teaspoon garlic salt

1 package (14 ounces) firm tofu, cut into 1/2-inch cubes

2 roma (plum) tomatoes, thinly sliced

1 hard-cooked egg, chopped

1 Heat oil in 12-inch skillet over medium-high heat. Cook onion in oil 2 minutes, stirring frequently. Stir in potatoes; reduce heat to medium-low. Cover and cook about 10 minutes, stirring occasionally, until potatoes are tender.

2 Stir in green beans, Italian seasoning and garlic salt. Cover and cook about 6 minutes, stirring occasionally, until beans are tender and potatoes are light golden brown.

3 Stir in tofu and tomatoes. Cook 2 to 3 minutes, stirring occasionally and gently, just until hot. Sprinkle each serving with egg.

1 SERVING: Calories 315

Fiber 5g	Sodium 230mg
Fat 16g	
(Saturated 2g)	Protein 18g
Cholesterol 55mg	Carbohydrate 30g

Food Exchanges: 1 Starch; 1 1/2 Lean Meat; 2 Vegetable; 2 Fat

Potato-Tomato-Tofu Dinner

Chapter 6

Sustaining Soups and Stews

Whether they're hearty or soothing, soups and stews can nourish your body and soul. Add breadsticks, a whole-wheat roll or whole-grain crackers and you're on your way to a delicious, sustaining meal.

1-1½
Carbohydrate Choices

Asian Pork and Noodle Soup 180

Beef 'n Veggie Soup with Mozzarella 175

Cream of Broccoli Soup 190

—— 1½ ——

Beef-Barley Stew 176

Cheesy Chicken-Pasta Stew 171

Split Pea Soup 183

Zesty Autumn Pork Stew 178

2
Carbohydrate Choices

Rio Grande Turkey Soup 174

Taco-Corn Chili 182

Tomato-Lentil Soup 186

Tortellini-Corn Chowder 188

White Chili 170

2½
Carbohydrate Choices

Black Bean and Salsa Noodle Soup 184

Smashed Potato Stew 191

Southwest Chicken Soup with Baked Tortilla Strips 172

3
Carbohydrate Choices

Easy Cheesy Vegetable Soup 189

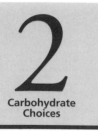

2

Carbohydrate
Choices

PREP: **30 min**

COOK: **25 min**

White Chili

6 servings

1 tablespoon canola or vegetable oil

1 large onion, chopped (1 cup)

2 cloves garlic, finely chopped

3 cups chicken broth

2 tablespoons chopped fresh cilantro or 1/2 teaspoon ground coriander

2 tablespoons lime juice

1 teaspoon ground cumin

1/2 teaspoon dried oregano leaves

1 can (15 to 16 ounces) great northern beans, drained

1 can (15 to 16 ounces) butter beans, drained

2 cups chopped cooked chicken or turkey breast

1 Heat oil in 4-quart Dutch oven over medium heat. Cook onion and garlic in oil, stirring occasionally, until onion is tender.

2 Stir in remaining ingredients except chicken. Heat to boiling; reduce heat. Simmer uncovered 20 minutes. Stir in chicken; simmer until hot.

1 SERVING: Calories 280

Fiber 10g	Sodium 710mg
Fat 6g	
(Saturated 1g)	Protein 30g
Cholesterol 40mg	Carbohydrate 36g

Food Exchanges: 2 Starch; 3 Very Lean Meat

Cheesy Chicken-Pasta Stew

PREP: **5 min**
COOK: **20 min**

5 servings

1 tablespoon canola oil or butter

1 pound boneless, skinless chicken breasts, cut into 1-inch pieces

1 cup fat-free (skim) milk

1 package (3 ounces) cream cheese, softened

1 bag (1 pound) frozen pasta, broccoli and carrots in creamy Cheddar sauce

2 tablespoons chopped fresh chives or green onions

1 Heat oil in 12-inch nonstick skillet over medium-high heat. Cook chicken in butter 4 to 5 minutes, stirring occasionally, until brown.

2 Stir in milk and cream cheese. Cook, stirring frequently, until cheese is melted.

3 Stir in frozen pasta and vegetable mixture. Heat to boiling, stirring occasionally; reduce heat. Cover and simmer 3 to 7 minutes or until pasta and vegetables are tender. Sprinkle with chives or green onions.

note from **DR. B**
Your doctor needs data to make important medication decisions; so remember to bring your blood glucose readings and your list of medications to your appointments.

1 SERVING: Calories 325

Fiber 2g	Sodium 440mg
Fat 15g (Saturated 8g)	Protein 27g
Cholesterol 80mg	Carbohydrate 21g

Food Exchanges: 1 Starch; 3 Lean Meat; 1 Vegetable;1 Fat

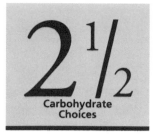

"I'm trying to eat more vegetables, and an easy way to do that is to include them in this slow cooker soup. Other tricks: I bring baby carrots, cucumber slices and celery sticks to eat while I'm waiting for the bus."
—PAT A.

PREP: **15 min**

COOK: **8 hr + 30 min**

note from **DR. B**

Sweet potatoes, squash, carrots and other bright orange vegetables contain beta-carotene, which your body converts to vitamin A. It's vital for proper eyesight and healthy hair and skin.

Southwest Chicken Soup with Baked Tortilla Strips

6 servings

1 pound boneless, skinless chicken thighs, cut into 1-inch pieces

2 medium sweet potatoes, peeled and cut into 1-inch pieces (2 cups)

1 large onion, chopped (1 cup)

2 cans (14 1/2 ounces each) diced tomatoes with green chilies, undrained

1 can (14 ounces) chicken broth

1 teaspoon dried oregano leaves

1/2 teaspoon ground cumin

1 cup frozen whole kernel corn

1/2 cup chopped green bell pepper

Baked Tortilla Strips (below)

2 tablespoons chopped fresh cilantro

1 Mix chicken, sweet potatoes, onion, tomatoes, broth, oregano and cumin in 3 1/2- to 4-quart slow cooker.

2 Cover and cook on low heat setting 7 to 8 hours. Stir in corn and bell pepper. Cover and cook on high heat setting about 30 minutes or until chicken is no longer pink in center and vegetables are tender.

3 Meanwhile, make Baked Tortilla Strips. Spoon soup into individual bowls. Top with tortilla strips. Sprinkle with cilantro.

Baked Tortilla Strips

8 yellow or blue corn tortillas (5 or 6 inches in diameter)

Heat oven to 450°. Spray 2 cookie sheets with cooking spray. Cut each tortilla into strips. Place in single layer on cookie sheets. Bake about 6 minutes or until crisp but not brown; cool.

1 SERVING: Calories 295

Fiber 5g	Sodium 770mg
Fat 7g (Saturated 2g)	Protein 22g
Cholesterol 45mg	Carbohydrate 41g

Food Exchanges: 2 Starch; 2 Lean Meat; 1 Vegetable

Southwest Chicken Soup with Baked Tortilla Strips

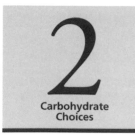

2
Carbohydrate
Choices

PREP: **5 min**

COOK: **15 min**

"There's enough spice in the salsa and chili powder to give this soup great flavor, so I use low-sodium, low-fat chicken broth to save on calories, fat and sodium."

—*PAT A.*

Rio Grande Turkey Soup

6 servings

1 can (14 ounces)
chicken broth

1 can (28 ounces) whole
tomatoes, undrained

1 jar (16 ounces) thick-and-chunky salsa

2 to 3 teaspoons chili powder

1/2 bag (1-pound size)
frozen corn, broccoli and
red peppers (or other
combination)

1 cup uncooked cavatappi
pasta (3 ounces)

2 cups cut-up cooked turkey
or chicken

1/4 cup chopped fresh parsley

1 Heat broth, tomatoes, salsa and chili powder to boiling in 4-quart Dutch oven, breaking up tomatoes. Stir in frozen vegetables and pasta. Heat to boiling; reduce heat.

2 Simmer uncovered about 12 minutes, stirring occasionally, until pasta and vegetables are tender. Stir in turkey and parsley; simmer until hot.

1 SERVING: Calories 255

Fiber 4g	Sodium 900mg
Fat 6g (Saturated 2g)	
	Protein 26g
Cholesterol 60mg	Carbohydrate 26g

Food Exchanges: 1 Starch;
3 Very Lean Meat; 2 Vegetable

"Diabetes affects the entire household, between diet and lifestyle changes. Feeling that you have enough support in caring for your diabetes is key."

—KATE D.

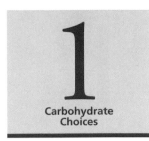

1

Carbohydrate Choices

PREP: **10 min**
COOK: **20 min**

Beef 'n Veggie Soup with Mozzarella

6 servings

1 pound extra-lean ground beef

1 large onion, chopped (1 cup)

1 can (14 1/2 ounces) diced tomatoes with green pepper, celery and onions, undrained

1 package (10 ounces) frozen mixed vegetables

4 cups water

1 tablespoon beef bouillon granules

1 1/2 teaspoons Italian seasoning

1/4 teaspoon pepper

1 cup shredded mozzarella cheese (4 ounces)

1 Cook beef and onion in 4-quart Dutch oven over medium-high heat, stirring occasionally, until beef is brown; drain.

2 Stir in remaining ingredients except cheese. Heat to boiling; reduce heat. Simmer uncovered 6 to 8 minutes, stirring occasionally, until vegetables are tender.

3 Sprinkle cheese in each of 6 soup bowls; fill bowls with soup.

note from **DR. B**

You can learn stress management techniques to avoid overeating during stressful times. Deep breathing exercises, yoga and meditation have all been found to be very helpful. Seek out help at community centers, gyms or on the web.

1 SERVING: Calories 230

Fiber 2g	Sodium 950mg
Fat 14g (Saturated 6g)	Protein 20g
Cholesterol 50mg	Carbohydrate 11g

Food Exchanges: 2 Medium-Fat Meat; 2 Vegetable

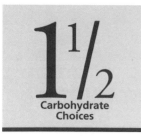

1½

Carbohydrate
Choices

PREP: **15 min**
BAKE: **1 hr 10 min**

"Cold, damp and dark weather can't dampen this winner! This stew is perfect for a football get-together or to bring to a friend in need." —MICHELLE M.

Beef-Barley Stew

6 servings

1 pound extra-lean ground beef

1 medium onion, chopped (1/2 cup)

2 cups beef broth

2/3 cup uncooked barley

2 teaspoons chopped fresh or 1/2 teaspoon dried oregano leaves

1/4 teaspoon salt

1/4 teaspoon pepper

1 can (14 1/2 ounces) whole tomatoes, undrained

1 can (8 ounces) sliced water chestnuts, undrained

1 package (10 ounces) frozen mixed vegetables

1 Heat oven to 350°. Spray 10-inch nonstick skillet with cooking spray. Cook beef and onion in skillet over medium heat 7 to 8 minutes, stirring occasionally, until beef is brown; drain.

2 Mix beef mixture and remaining ingredients except frozen vegetables in ungreased 3-quart casserole, breaking up tomatoes.

3 Cover and bake 30 minutes. Stir in frozen vegetables. Cover and bake 30 to 40 minutes longer or until barley is tender.

1 SERVING: Calories 250

Fiber 6g	Sodium 600mg
Fat 9g (Saturated 3g)	Protein 20g
Cholesterol 45mg	Carbohydrate 29g

Food Exchanges: 1 Starch; 2 Lean Meat; 2 Vegetable

**Beef-Barley Stew and Parmesan-Herb Breadsticks
(page 69)**

"Heart disease runs in my family, and my doctor says that people with diabetes are at extra risk. So, besides watching carbohydrates, I'm keeping the total amount of fat that I eat low. This recipe is a great low-fat choice." —SHERRY L.

PREP: **10 min**
COOK: **20 min**

Betty's **success tip**

Comfort foods, such as stew, are really satisfying. Savor hearty stews, creamy mashed potatoes and any other food that brings you comfort and fits in your food plan. Take the time to enjoy every moment of your meal.

Zesty Autumn Pork Stew

4 servings

1 pound pork tenderloin

2 cloves garlic,
finely chopped

2 medium sweet potatoes,
peeled and cubed (2 cups)

1 medium green bell pepper,
chopped (1 cup)

1 cup coarsely chopped
cabbage

1 teaspoon Cajun seasoning

1 can (14 ounces)
chicken broth

1 Remove fat from pork. Cut pork into 1-inch cubes. Spray 4-quart Dutch oven with cooking spray; heat over medium-high heat. Cook pork in Dutch oven, stirring occasionally, until brown, about 5 minutes.

2 Stir in remaining ingredients. Heat to boiling; reduce heat. Cover and simmer about 15 minutes, stirring once, until sweet potatoes are tender.

1 SERVING: Calories 240

Fiber 3g   Sodium
                820mg
Fat 5g
(Saturated 2g) Protein 30g

Cholesterol   Carbohydrate
70mg   22g

Food Exchanges: 1 Starch;
3 Very Lean Meat; 1 Vegetable

Fiber Boosters

It's a fact: most people don't eat enough fiber. Sometimes it's just easier to grab fruit juice instead of whole fruit, chips instead of vegetables, or white bread instead of whole wheat. And yet, fiber is so important for keeping the body regulated.

Fiber offers many health benefits. Since it's basically roughage, fiber provides a sense of fullness without the calories and satisfies your appetite without affecting your blood glucose levels. If you eat a food with 5 or more grams of fiber, you can subtract the fiber from the total grams of carbohydrate in the food. This calculation was done for the recipes in this cookbook. Choose foods high in fiber when you can—it will make sticking to your meal plan easier. Add fiber in these great ways:

- *Introduce it.* Slowly adding high-fiber cereal, such as Fiber One, to your diet each day (until you reach up to 1/2 cup) will allow your body time to adjust. ***Remember to drink extra liquids, because fiber acts like a sponge in the intestines.***

- *Don't skin it.* The skins, seeds and hulls found in fruits, vegetables and grains are fiber. Eat pears, apples, peaches, potatoes and other fruits and vegetables with the skin. If they're too hard for you to bite into, use a knife to cut them into sections.

- *Top it.* When eating salads and soups, top with high-fiber cereals, popcorn or wheat germ. For pancakes, waffles or toast, use fruit sauces with seeds, such as raspberries, strawberries or kiwi, for topping.

- *Distribute it.* Eating fiber-rich foods throughout the day will help you achieve your goal. Start the day by eating a banana for breakfast, a pear with lunch, baby carrots for a snack, green beans for dinner. Aim for at least five servings of fruits or vegetables a day.

- *Stuff it.* Place tomato slices, shredded cabbage, sliced bell peppers and spinach leaves between slices of whole-grain bread. Whole wheat pita, whole-grain breadsticks and whole-grain crackers are also fiber rich.

- *Combine it.* Have high-fiber cereal with strawberries for breakfast, a whole-wheat bread sandwich with veggies for lunch and vegetable or split pea soup with whole-grain crackers for dinner.

- *Bake it.* When baking, add fiber cereals, such as Fiber One, or bran to muffins, cookies and snack mixes.

- *Snack it.* Snack on fiber-rich foods such as high-fiber cereal, air-popped popcorn, raw vegetables, nuts and soy nuts, raisins or other dried fruit.

PREP: **10 min**

COOK: **20 min**

Asian Pork and Noodle Soup

5 servings

**1 pound pork boneless sirloin
or loin, cut into 1/2-inch
pieces**

**2 cloves garlic,
finely chopped**

**2 teaspoons finely chopped
gingerroot**

**2 cans (14 ounces each)
chicken broth**

2 cups water

2 tablespoons soy sauce

**2 cups uncooked fine
egg noodles (4 ounces)**

**1 medium carrot, sliced
(1/2 cup)**

**1 small red bell pepper,
chopped (1/2 cup)**

2 cups fresh spinach leaves

1 Spray 3-quart saucepan with cooking spray; heat over
medium-high heat. Add pork, garlic and gingerroot;
stir-fry 3 to 5 minutes or until pork is brown.

2 Stir in broth, water and soy sauce. Heat to boiling; reduce
heat. Simmer uncovered 5 minutes. Stir in noodles, carrot
and bell pepper. Simmer uncovered about 10 minutes or
until noodles are tender.

3 Stir in spinach; cook until heated through.

1 SERVING: Calories 235

Fiber 2g	Sodium 1160mg
Fat 9g (Saturated 3g)	Protein 26g
Cholesterol 70mg	Carbohydrate 15g

Food Exchanges: 1 Starch;
3 Very Lean Meat; 1 Fat

Asian Pork and Noodle Soup and
Hearty Multigrain Biscuits (page 71)

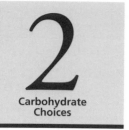

2
Carbohydrate Choices

PREP: **5 min**
COOK: **25 min**

note from **DR. B**

Though this recipe appears high in carbohydrates at first glance, it contains over 5 grams of fiber. To calculate the Carbohydrate Choices, first, subtract the total grams of fiber from the total carbohydrate, then use the *How Many Carbohydrate Choices?* conversion guide (page 12). You'll see that this recipe counts as only 34 grams of carbohydrate and 2 Choices.

"When I can't find extra-lean pork, I substitute extra-lean beef, turkey or chicken."
—LORI S.

Taco-Corn Chili

5 servings

1 pound extra-lean ground pork

1 can (15 to 16 ounces) kidney beans, rinsed and drained

1 envelope (1 1/4 ounces) taco seasoning mix

1 can (10 ounces) diced tomatoes and green chilies, undrained

1 package (10 ounces) frozen whole kernel corn, thawed and drained

2 cups water

2 teaspoons sugar

1 Spray 4-quart Dutch oven with cooking spray; heat over medium-high heat. Cook pork in Dutch oven, stirring occasionally, until no longer pink; drain.

2 Stir in remaining ingredients. Heat to boiling; reduce heat. Simmer uncovered 18 minutes, stirring occasionally.

1 SERVING: Calories 255

Fiber 10g
Fat 8g
(Saturated 3g)
Cholesterol 70mg

Sodium 620mg
Protein 18g
Carbohydrate 44g

Food Exchanges: 2 Starch; 1 1/2 Lean Meat; 1 Vegetable

"I always keep sunshine in my thoughts, even on a cloudy day. It helps keep my disposition on an even keel."
—SHERRY L.

Split Pea Soup

8 servings

PREP: **20 min**
COOK: **2 hr**

2 1/4 cups dried split peas (1 pound), sorted and rinsed

8 cups water

1/4 teaspoon pepper

1 large onion, chopped (1 cup)

2 medium stalks celery, finely chopped (1 cup)

1 ham bone, 2 pounds ham shanks or 2 pounds smoked pork hocks

3 medium carrots, cut into 1/4-inch slices (1 1/2 cups)

1 Heat all ingredients except carrots to boiling in 4-quart Dutch oven, stirring occasionally; reduce heat. Cover and simmer 1 hour to 1 hour 30 minutes.

2 Remove ham bone; let stand until cool enough to handle. Remove ham from bone. Remove excess fat from ham; cut ham into 1/2-inch pieces.

3 Stir ham and carrots into soup. Heat to boiling; reduce heat. Cover and simmer about 30 minutes or until carrots are tender and soup is desired consistency.

Betty's **success tip**

Split peas, a variety of pea grown specifically for drying and cooking, are found with the dried beans and lentils in the supermarket. Split peas are high in fiber; in fact, just one serving of this soup gives you one-third of the fiber you need for the day.

1 SERVING: Calories 190

Fiber 12g	Sodium 210mg
Fat 5g (Saturated 2g)	Protein 16g
Cholesterol 15mg	Carbohydrate 33g

Food Exchanges: 1 Starch; 1 1/2 Very Lean Meat; 1 Vegetable

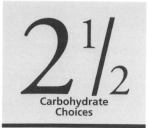

2¹/₂

Carbohydrate Choices

PREP: **10 min**

COOK: **10 min**

note from **DR. B**

Whenever you see a soup, salad or main dish made with beans, rest assured that it's full of vitamins, minerals and especially the fiber that's so important to good blood glucose management.

Black Bean and Salsa Noodle Soup

6 servings

2 cans (14 ounces each) vegetable broth

1 cup water

1 jar (16 ounces) salsa

1 can (15 ounces) black beans, rinsed and drained

1 package (5 ounces) Japanese curly noodles or 5 ounces uncooked spaghetti

1/3 cup chopped fresh cilantro

1 tablespoon lime juice

1 teaspoon chili powder

1/4 teaspoon ground cumin

1/4 teaspoon pepper

2 tablespoons shredded Parmesan cheese

1 Heat broth to boiling in 4-quart Dutch oven. Stir in remaining ingredients except cheese; reduce heat to medium.

2 Cook 5 to 6 minutes, stirring occasionally, until noodles are tender. Sprinkle with cheese.

1 SERVING: Calories 210

Fiber 7g	Sodium 1240mg
Fat 2g (Saturated 1g)	Protein 11g
Cholesterol 0mg	Carbohydrate 44g

Food Exchanges: 2 Starch; 1 1/2 Vegetable

Free Foods

A free food is any food or drink that contains less than 5 grams of carbohydrate and less than 20 calories per serving. Limit foods with a specific serving size listed below to three servings per day. If you choose to eat three servings of any of these foods, spread the servings throughout the day. You can eat any foods listed without a serving size as often as desired.

Sugar-Free or Low-Sugar

- Candy, hard, sugar-free, 1 candy
- Gelatin, unflavored
- Gelatin dessert, sugar-free
- Gum, sugar-free
- Jam or jelly, low-sugar or light, 2 teaspoons
- Sugar substitutes
- Syrup, sugar-free, 2 tablespoons

Condiments

- Horseradish
- Ketchup, 1 tablespoon
- Lemon or lime juice
- Mustard
- Pickles, dill, 1 1/2 large
- Soy sauce, regular or light
- Taco sauce
- Vinegar

Drinks

- Bouillon, broth or consommé
- Carbonated or mineral water
- Club soda or tonic water, sugar-free
- Hot cocoa powder, unsweetened
- Coffee and tea
- Soft drinks, sugar-free
- Drink mixes, sugar-free

Fat-Free or Reduced-Fat

- Cream cheese, fat-free, 1 tablespoon
- Creamers, nondairy, liquid, 1 tablespoon or powdered, 2 teaspoons
- Margarine, reduced-fat, 1 teaspoon
- Mayonnaise, fat-free, 1 tablespoon or reduced-fat, 1 teaspoon
- Mayonnaise-type salad dressing, fat-free, 1 tablespoon or reduced-fat, 1 teaspoon
- Nonstick cooking spray
- Salad dressing, fat-free, 1 tablespoon

Seasonings

- Flavor extracts
- Garlic
- Herbs, fresh or dried
- Pimiento
- Red pepper sauce
- Spices
- Wine, used in cooking
- Worcestershire sauce

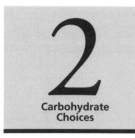

2

Carbohydrate
Choices

PREP: **10 min**

COOK: **40 min**

Betty's **success tip**

Lentils are so wholesome. They're low in calories and a good source of fiber, plus they're low in fat. Lentils are available in a variety of colors, including grayish brown (the most widely available), yellow and red. Use your favorite type of lentil in this easy soup.

1 SERVING: Calories 210

Fiber 14g	Sodium 950mg
Fat 4g	
(Saturated 1g)	Protein 15g
Cholesterol 0mg	Carbohydrate 43g

Food Exchanges: 1 Starch; 1 Very Lean Meat; 2 Vegetable

"Filled with onion, celery, carrots, lentils and tomatoes, this soup provides a wholesome base for a vegetarian meal. It's perfect for our diabetic daughter."

—*Betty H.*

Tomato-Lentil Soup

4 servings

1 tablespoon olive or
canola oil

1 large onion, finely chopped
(1 cup)

1 medium stalk celery,
cut into 1/2-inch pieces
(1/2 cup)

2 cloves garlic,
finely chopped

2 medium carrots, cut into
1/2-inch pieces (1 cup)

1 cup dried lentils (8 ounces),
sorted and rinsed

4 cups water

2 teaspoons chicken or
vegetable bouillon granules

1 teaspoon dried
thyme leaves

1/4 teaspoon pepper

1 dried bay leaf

1 can (28 ounces) diced
tomatoes, undrained

1 Heat oil in 3-quart saucepan over medium-high heat. Cook onion, celery and garlic in oil about 5 minutes, stirring occasionally, until softened.

2 Stir in remaining ingredients except tomatoes. Heat to boiling; reduce heat. Cover and simmer 15 to 20 minutes or until lentils and vegetables are tender.

3 Stir in tomatoes. Simmer uncovered about 15 minutes or until heated through. Remove bay leaf.

Tomato-Lentil Soup

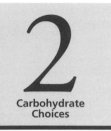
PREP: **8 min**

COOK: **25 min**

Tortellini-Corn Chowder

8 servings

1 tablespoon canola oil or butter

1 large onion, chopped (1 cup)

3 cups water

1 package (9 ounces) refrigerated cheese-filled tortellini

2 medium unpeeled potatoes, cut into 1/2-inch cubes

1/2 pound fully cooked ham, cut into 1/2-inch pieces (about 1 1/3 cups)

1 can (15 ounces) cream-style corn

1 can (11 ounces) whole kernel corn with red and green peppers, undrained

1 can (12 ounces) evaporated milk

2 teaspoons chopped fresh or 1 teaspoon dried marjoram leaves

1/4 teaspoon coarsely ground pepper

1 Heat oil in 4-quart Dutch oven over medium heat. Cook onion in oil, stirring occasionally, until tender.

2 Stir in water; heat to boiling. Stir in tortellini and potatoes. Heat to boiling; reduce heat. Cover and simmer 13 to 15 minutes, stirring occasionally, until potatoes are tender.

3 Stir in remaining ingredients. Heat to boiling; reduce heat. Simmer uncovered 5 minutes.

Betty's **success tip**

This is a great soup for entertaining or toting to a potluck supper. You still have a couple of Carbohydrate Choices to play with, because this soup has only 2. How about serving with a crisp, green salad and Parmesan-Herb Breadsticks (page 69)? You may even be able to have a 1-Carb-Choice dessert, perhaps a Key Lime Bar (page 222) or Oatmeal Brownie (page 223).

1 SERVING: Calories 270

Fiber 3g	Sodium 710mg
Fat 9g (Saturated 4g)	Protein 15g
Cholesterol 55mg	Carbohydrate 35g

Food Exchanges: 2 Starch; 1 Lean Meat; 1 Vegetable; 1 Fat

Easy Cheesy Vegetable Soup

5 servings

PREP: **5 min**

COOK: **10 min**

4 ounces reduced-fat process
cheese spread loaf, cubed

3 1/2 cups fat-free (skim) milk

1/2 teaspoon chili powder

2 cups cooked brown or
white rice

1 bag (1 pound) frozen
cauliflower, carrots and
asparagus (or other
combination), thawed
and drained

1 Heat cheese and milk in 3-quart saucepan over low heat,
stirring occasionally, until cheese is melted.

2 Stir in chili powder. Stir in rice and vegetables; cook until hot.

Betty's **success tip**

Be ready to make this
soup anytime by
cooking your favorite
rice ahead of time.
Store cooked rice in
an airtight container
or resealable plastic
food-storage bag in
the refrigerator up to
5 days or in the freezer
up to 6 months.

1 SERVING: Calories 255

Fiber 4g	Sodium 460mg
Fat 4g (Saturated 2g)	Protein 15g
Cholesterol 10mg	Carbohydrate 44g

Food Exchanges: 2 Starch;
2 Vegetable; 1/2 Skim Milk

Carbohydrate Choices

PREP: **10 min**
COOK: **20 min**

note from **DR. B**

Good diabetes care requires regular monitoring. Schedule appointments with your diabetes care team at least two times per year, or as often as your doctor recommends.

"I am always trying to make my life easier, so I use two 10-ounce packages of frozen chopped broccoli, without thawing, and low-sodium, low-fat chicken broth in this tasty soup."
—PAT A.

Cream of Broccoli Soup

4 servings

2 tablespoons canola oil or butter

1 medium onion, chopped (1/2 cup)

2 medium carrots, thinly sliced (1 cup)

2 teaspoons mustard seed

1/2 teaspoon salt

1/4 teaspoon pepper

3/4 pound broccoli, coarsely chopped (3 1/2 cups)

1 can (14 ounces) chicken broth

1 cup water

2 teaspoons lemon juice

1/4 cup sour cream

1 Heat oil in 3-quart saucepan over medium heat. Cook onion and carrots in oil about 5 minutes, stirring occasionally, until onion is tender. Stir in mustard seed, salt and pepper. Stir in broccoli, broth and water. Heat to boiling; reduce heat. Cover and simmer about 10 minutes or until broccoli is tender.

2 Place one-third of the broccoli mixture in blender. Cover and blend on high speed until smooth; pour into bowl. Continue to blend in small batches until all soup is pureed.

3 Return blended soup to saucepan. Stir in lemon juice. Heat over low heat just until hot. Stir in sour cream.

1 SERVING: Calories 140

Fiber 4g	Sodium 840mg
Fat 10g (Saturated 6g)	Protein 6g
Cholesterol 25mg	Carbohydrate 11g

Food Exchanges: 2 Vegetable; 2 Fat

Smashed Potato Stew

$2\frac{1}{2}$ Carbohydrate Choices

PREP: **10 min**
COOK: **20 min**

6 servings

3 1/2 cups fat-free (skim) milk

3 tablespoons all-purpose flour

1 tablespoon canola oil or butter

1 large onion, finely chopped (1 cup)

4 medium unpeeled potatoes (1 1/2 pounds), cut into 1/4-inch pieces

1 teaspoon salt

1/4 teaspoon black pepper

1/8 teaspoon ground red pepper (cayenne)

1 1/2 cups shredded reduced-fat sharp Cheddar cheese (6 ounces)

1/3 cup reduced-fat sour cream

8 medium green onions, sliced (1/2 cup)

1 Beat 1/2 cup of the milk and the flour with wire whisk until smooth; set aside. Heat oil in 4-quart Dutch oven over medium heat. Cook onion in oil about 2 minutes, stirring occasionally, until tender. Increase heat to high; stir in remaining 3 cups milk.

2 Stir in potatoes, salt, black pepper and red pepper. Heat to boiling; reduce heat. Simmer uncovered 15 to 16 minutes, stirring frequently, until potatoes are tender.

3 Beat in flour mixture with wire whisk. Cook about 2 minutes, stirring frequently, until thickened; remove from heat. Beat potato mixture with wire whisk until potatoes are slightly mashed. Stir in cheese, sour cream and green onions.

Betty's **success tip**

This stew is so thick and creamy, you'll want to make it the star of your meal. At 2 1/2 Carbohydrate Choices, you could partner it with a slice of crusty French bread and a fresh garden salad for a stick-to-your-ribs dinner.

1 SERVING: Calories 230

Fiber 3g	Sodium 670mg
Fat 4g (Saturated 3g)	Protein 16g
Cholesterol 15mg	Carbohydrate 36g

Food Exchanges: 2 Starch; 1/2 Skim Milk; 1 Very Lean Meat

7 Valuable Vegetables and Salads

Virtuous, delicious vegetables contribute vitally important fiber, vitamins and minerals and low carbohydrates to your good health. To hype your veggie excitement, try plenty of new recipes.

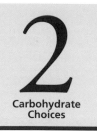

2

Carbohydrate
Choices

PREP: **10 min**

COOK: **30 min**

STAND: **5 min**

"I prefer to use Yukon gold potatoes because they don't raise my blood sugar quite as high as white potatoes do."
—SAMMY E.

Rosemary-Parmesan Mashers

6 servings

6 medium Yukon gold potatoes (2 pounds)

1/3 to 1/2 cup chicken broth

2 tablespoons olive or canola oil

1 teaspoon chopped fresh or 1/4 teaspoon dried rosemary leaves, crumbled

1/4 teaspoon salt

1/3 cup shredded Parmesan cheese

1 Place potatoes in 2-quart saucepan; add enough water just to cover potatoes. Heat to boiling; reduce heat. Cover and simmer 20 to 30 minutes or until potatoes are tender; drain. Shake pan with potatoes over low heat to dry (this will help mashed potatoes be fluffier).

2 Mash potatoes in pan until no lumps remain. Add broth in small amounts, mashing after each addition (amount of broth needed to make potatoes smooth and fluffy will vary).

3 Add oil, rosemary, salt and cheese. Mash vigorously until potatoes are light and fluffy. Cover and let stand 5 minutes. Sprinkle with additional rosemary and Parmesan cheese if desired.

1 SERVING: Calories 180

Fiber 3g	Sodium 260mg
Fat 6g (Saturated 2g)	Protein 5g
Cholesterol 5mg	Carbohydrate 30g

Food Exchanges: 2 Starch; 1 Fat

"I like to serve this side with a pork dish and just add a fresh salad for a great 'balanced' meal!"
—LORI S.

Caramelized Onion and Sweet Potato Skillet

4 servings

1 teaspoon canola or vegetable oil

1/4 large sweet onion (such as Bermuda, Maui, Spanish or Vidalia), sliced

3 medium sweet potatoes, peeled and sliced (3 1/2 cups)

2 tablespoons packed brown sugar

1/2 teaspoon jerk seasoning (dry)

1 tablespoon chopped fresh parsley

1 Heat oil in 10-inch skillet over medium heat. Cook onion and sweet potatoes in oil about 5 minutes, stirring occasionally, until light brown; reduce heat to low. Cover and cook 10 to 12 minutes, stirring occasionally, until potatoes are tender.

2 Stir in brown sugar and jerk seasoning. Cook uncovered about 3 minutes, stirring occasionally, until glazed. Sprinkle with parsley.

PREP: **10 min**

COOK: **20 min**

note from **DR. B**
Though only 3 to 5 percent of pregnant women develop gestational diabetes, all pregnant women should have a blood glucose screening between the twenty-fourth and twenty-eighth weeks of pregnancy. Some women can't make enough insulin during pregnancy to keep blood glucose levels normal, which is important for the health of both mother and baby.

1 SERVING: Calories 115

Fiber 3g	Sodium 300mg
Fat 1g (Saturated 0g)	Protein 2g
Cholesterol 0mg	Carbohydrate 28g

Food Exchanges: 2 Starch

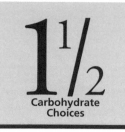

1½
Carbohydrate
Choices

PREP: **10 min**

BAKE: **30 min**

"I know fries are not good for my diabetes; I don't need all that oil. These potatoes are a great alternative!"
—Tᴍ *H.*

Oven-Fried Potato Wedges

4 servings

3/4 teaspoon salt

1/2 teaspoon sugar

1/2 teaspoon paprika

1/4 teaspoon ground mustard

1/4 teaspoon garlic powder

3 medium baking potatoes
(8 to 10 ounces each)

Cooking spray

1 Heat oven to 425°. Mix salt, sugar, paprika, mustard and garlic powder.

2 Gently scrub potatoes, but do not peel. Cut each potato lengthwise in half; cut each half lengthwise into 4 wedges. Place potato wedges, skin sides down, in ungreased rectangular pan, 13 × 9 × 2 inches.

3 Spray potatoes with cooking spray until lightly coated. Sprinkle with salt mixture. Bake uncovered 25 to 30 minutes or until potatoes are tender when pierced with fork. (Baking time will vary depending on the size and type of the potato used.)

1 SERVING: Calories 105

Fiber 2g	Sodium 450mg
Fat 0g (Saturated 0g)	Protein 2g
Cholesterol 0mg	Carbohydrate 24g

Food Exchanges: 1 1/2 Starch

**Oven-Fried Potato Wedges and Pizza Burgers
(page 122)**

O

Carbohydrate
Choices

PREP: **10 min**

BROIL: **12 min**

Betty's **success tip**

This easy-to-fix veggie sidekick is ideal for hectic schedules because it cooks so quickly. Serve with grilled fish or chicken, or use it to top a baked potato or a serving of pasta for a virtually effortless meal.

"After living with diabetes for years, I've really come to love vegetables because they help 'regulate' my blood glucose levels. I can still eat a slice of pizza with these great veggies, as long as I keep my total Carbohydrate Choices to 4."

—*LORI S.*

Harvest Roasted Vegetables

4 servings

1 medium green bell pepper, cut into 1-inch pieces

1 medium onion, cut into 1/4-inch wedges

1 medium tomato, cut into 1/4-inch wedges

1 medium zucchini, cut into 1-inch pieces

Olive oil–flavored cooking spray

1/2 teaspoon salt

1 Set oven control to broil. Cover cookie sheet with aluminum foil; spray with cooking spray. Place vegetables in single layer on cookie sheet. Spray vegetables with cooking spray. Sprinkle with 1/4 teaspoon of the salt.

2 Broil with tops 4 inches from heat about 12 minutes, stirring occasionally, until vegetables are tender. Sprinkle with remaining 1/4 teaspoon salt.

1 SERVING: Calories 30

Fiber 2g

Fat 0g
(Saturated 0g)

Cholesterol
0mg

Sodium
300mg

Protein 1g

Carbohydrate
7g

Food Exchanges: 1 Vegetable

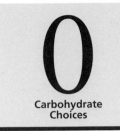

0
Carbohydrate
Choices

PREP: **15 min**
COOK: **10 min**

Broccoli and Tomatoes with Herbs

4 servings

1 pound broccoli, cut into flowerets and stems cut into 1 × 1/2-inch pieces (4 cups)*

2 tablespoons olive or canola oil

1 teaspoon chopped fresh or 1/4 teaspoon dried basil leaves

1 teaspoon chopped fresh or 1/4 teaspoon dried oregano leaves

1/2 teaspoon salt

1 clove garlic, finely chopped

2 roma (plum) tomatoes, seeded and chopped

1 Heat 1 inch water to boiling in 10-inch skillet. Add broccoli. Heat to boiling. Boil 5 to 7 minutes or until crisp-tender; drain and set aside. Wipe out and dry skillet with paper towel.

2 Heat oil in same skillet over medium heat. Stir in remaining ingredients. Heat about 1 minute, stirring frequently, until hot. Add broccoli; toss gently.

* 2 packages (10 ounces each) frozen chopped broccoli, cooked and drained, can be substituted for the fresh broccoli. Omit step 1; cook broccoli as directed on package.

note from **DR. B**
Broccoli, in the cruciferous family of vegetables along with Brussels sprouts, cauliflower, cabbage and kale, is a nutrient powerhouse. Cruciferous vegetables are thought to protect against diseases, particularly certain kinds of cancer.

1 SERVING: Calories 75

Fiber 2g | Sodium 320mg
Fat 6g
(Saturated 1g) | Protein 2g
Cholesterol 0mg | Carbohydrate 5g

Food Exchanges: 1 Vegetable; 1 Fat

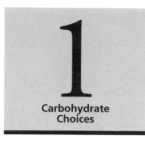

1

Carbohydrate
Choices

PREP: **15 min**

BAKE: **50 min**

Betty's **success tip**

Topping with a cereal that has nuts and dried fruit gives this squash sweetness and crunch. You can use Honey Nut Clusters or Harmony cereal instead, plus some dried raisins or cranberries.

"Everyone in our family loves squash so I make this all the time. Sometimes I use acorn squash instead and sprinkle different kinds of crunchy cereal on top."

—MICHELE H.

Nut- and Fruit-Filled Squash

4 servings

**1 buttercup squash
(2 to 2 1/2 pounds)**

1/4 teaspoon salt

1 tablespoon butter or margarine, melted

1 cup Basic 4 cereal, coarsely crushed (1/2 cup)

1 teaspoon grated orange peel

1 Heat oven to 350°. Cut squash into fourths; remove seeds and fibers. Place squash, cut sides up, in ungreased rectangular baking dish, 13 × 9 × 2 inches.

2 Sprinkle salt over squash. Pour water into baking dish until 1/4 inch deep. Cover and bake 40 to 50 minutes or until tender.

3 Mix butter, cereal and orange peel; spoon into squash.

1 SERVING: Calories 140

Fiber 6g	Sodium 250mg
Fat 5g (Saturated 2g)	Protein 3g
Cholesterol 5mg	Carbohydrate 26g

Food Exchanges: 1 Starch; 1 Fat

Nut- and Fruit-Filled Squash

PREP: **10 min**

MICROWAVE: **5 min**

Corn- and Pepper-Stuffed Zucchini

4 servings

**4 small zucchini
(about 6 inches long)**

1 tablespoon water

3/4 cup frozen (thawed) whole kernel corn or cooled cooked fresh corn kernels

2 tablespoons diced red bell pepper

1 tablespoon chopped fresh or 1/2 teaspoon dried basil leaves

2 medium green onions, thinly sliced (2 tablespoons)

2 teaspoons olive or canola oil

1/8 teaspoon salt

1 Cut zucchini lengthwise in half; place zucchini and water in rectangular microwavable dish, $11 \times 7 \times 1\ 1/2$ inches. Cover with plastic wrap, folding back one edge or corner 1/4 inch to vent steam.

2 Microwave on High 3 to 5 minutes or until zucchini is crisp-tender. When cool enough to handle, scoop centers from zucchini, leaving 1/4-inch shells. Discard centers.

3 Mix remaining ingredients. Spoon about 2 tablespoons corn mixture into each zucchini shell.

1 SERVING: Calories 65

Fiber 2g	Sodium 80mg
Fat 3g (Saturated 0g)	Protein 2g
	Carbohydrate 10g
Cholesterol 0mg	

Food Exchanges: 2 Vegetable; 1/2 Fat

The Value of Vegetables

When you have diabetes, knowing the many health benefits of vegetables is more important than ever. Veggies are colorful and fun, add fiber and important vitamins and minerals, and are naturally low in calories. To maximize your vegetable options:

- *Make vegetables fun.* Try dipping carrots, cucumber slices, celery and bell pepper strips into colorful low-fat dips.

- *Drink your veggies.* Try your hand at juicing, or if you'd rather, drink tomato, eight-vegetable or other vegetable juices.

- *Try new recipes with vegetables.* Adding a simple new low-fat sauce, topping with bread or cereal crumbs or teaming with other veggies creates interest and variety for everyone in the family.

- *Take advantage of convenience.* Buy baby carrots and pea pods to keep on hand for anytime snacking.

- *Keep fresh veggies at the ready.* Wash and cut broccoli, cucumbers, celery and bell peppers ahead of time. Place in individual storage bags to easily carry to work.

- *Add veggie variety to sandwiches.* Stuff lettuce leaves along with chicken chunks into pita breads; slice a cucumber or red bell pepper for your tuna sandwich; add tomato to your grilled cheese.

- *Top omelets, scrambled eggs and potato dishes.* Cooked onions, mushrooms, zucchini and bell peppers make great toppers.

- *Keep bagged salads on hand.* Or wash and dry lettuce, chop up other salad ingredients and keep in food-storage bags in refrigerator. Washed and well dried, salad greens will keep for several days.

- *Save leftover cooked vegetables.* Add them to soups, salads, egg dishes and casseroles.

- *Stock frozen and canned vegetables.* That way you'll always have vegetables on hand, even when you don't have time to shop.

A Rainbow of Colors

When it comes to choosing vegetables, looks do count! Choosing produce that's rich in color often means that it's rich in vitamins and other nutrients. When you're grocery shopping, include:

- **Dark green veggies such as broccoli, Brussels sprouts, spinach, romaine lettuce and asparagus**

- **Orange veggies such as carrots, sweet potatoes and winter squash**

- **Red veggies such as tomatoes, beets and radishes**

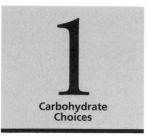

Carbohydrate Choices

PREP: **10 min**
COOK: **10 min**

note from **DR. B**

Corn and lima beans are the essential ingredients in a succotash. Lima beans are a good source of protein, phosphorus, potassium, iron and fiber.

Creamy Confetti Succotash

5 servings

1 tablespoon canola oil or butter

1 small red or green bell pepper, chopped (1/2 cup)

2 medium green onions, sliced (2 tablespoons)

2 cups fresh or frozen whole kernel corn

1 cup frozen baby lima beans

1/4 cup half-and-half

2 teaspoons chopped fresh or 1/2 teaspoon dried marjoram leaves

1/4 teaspoon salt

1/8 teaspoon pepper

1 Heat oil in 8-inch skillet over medium-high heat. Cook bell pepper and onions in oil 2 to 3 minutes, stirring occasionally, until crisp-tender.

2 Stir in remaining ingredients; reduce heat to medium-low. Cover and cook 5 to 6 minutes, stirring occasionally, until vegetables are tender.

1 SERVING: Calories 115

Fiber 4g	Sodium 160mg
Fat 4g (Saturated 2g)	Protein 4g
Cholesterol 10mg	Carbohydrate 20g

Food Exchanges: 1 Starch; 1 Vegetable; 1/2 Fat

Creamy Confetti Succotash and
Breaded Pork Chops (page 132)

PREP: **10 min**

CHILL: **3 hr**

note from **DR. B**

Tomatoes are a good source of lycopene, a phytochemical (or naturally occurring plant chemical in foods) that may have cancer-fighting properties.

"This delicious salad goes well with baked rigatoni and other pasta dishes."

—*BETTY H.*

Fresh Mozzarella and Tomatoes

8 servings

4 medium tomatoes, cut into 1/4-inch slices

1/4 cup olive or canola oil

1 tablespoon chopped fresh or 1 teaspoon dried basil leaves

3 tablespoons red wine vinegar

1 tablespoon water

1/8 teaspoon salt

3 drops red pepper sauce

2 large cloves garlic, finely chopped

8 ounces fresh mozzarella cheese, sliced

Salad greens, if desired

1 Place tomatoes in glass or plastic dish. Shake remaining ingredients except cheese and salad greens in tightly covered container; pour over tomatoes.

2 Cover and refrigerate, turning tomatoes occasionally, at least 3 hours to blend flavors. Layer tomatoes alternately with cheese on salad greens.

1 SERVING: Calories 150

Fiber 1g	Sodium 190mg
Fat 12g (Saturated 4g)	Protein 8g
Cholesterol 15mg	Carbohydrate 4g

Food Exchanges: 1 High-Fat Meat; 1 Vegetable; 1 Fat

"Whether I'm eating in or dining out, I love salads. They really fill me up without adding a lot of carbohydrates." —PAT A.

1
Carbohydrate
Choices

PREP: **10 min**
CHILL: **1 hr**

Mediterranean Vegetable Salad

6 servings

2 large yellow bell peppers, sliced into thin rings

3 large tomatoes, sliced

1/3 cup tarragon or white wine vinegar

3 tablespoons olive or canola oil

2 tablespoons chopped fresh or 2 teaspoons dried oregano leaves

1/2 teaspoon salt

1/2 teaspoon pepper

1/2 teaspoon sugar

1/2 teaspoon ground mustard

2 cloves garlic, finely chopped

6 ounces spinach leaves

1/2 cup crumbled feta cheese (2 ounces)

Kalamata olives, if desired

1 Place bell peppers and tomatoes in glass or plastic dish. Shake vinegar, oil, oregano, salt, pepper, sugar, mustard and garlic in tightly covered container. Pour vinegar mixture over vegetables. Cover and refrigerate at least 1 hour to blend flavors.

2 Line serving platter with spinach. Drain vegetables; place on spinach. Sprinkle with cheese. Garnish with olives.

note from **DR. B**
Vegetable salads are a great way to make a dent in your recommended three to five daily servings of fresh vegetables. With all the health benefits fresh veggies offer, some experts say you should aim for as many as seven to nine daily servings.

1 SERVING: Calories 140

Fiber 2g	Sodium 360mg
Fat 10g (Saturated 3g)	Protein 4g
Cholesterol 10mg	Carbohydrate 11g

Food Exchanges: 2 Vegetable; 2 Fat

PREP: **15 min**

CHILL: **2 hrs**

Layered Gazpacho Salad

9 servings

Lemon-Garlic Vinaigrette (below)

1 bag (8 ounces) Mediterranean lettuce blend

2 medium tomatoes, diced (2 cups)

2 medium cucumbers, diced (2 cups)

1 medium green bell pepper, chopped (1 cup)

1/2 cup finely chopped red onion

2 hard-cooked eggs, chopped

1 cup seasoned croutons

1 Make Lemon-Garlic Vinaigrette. Place lettuce in large glass bowl. Layer tomatoes, cucumbers, bell pepper and onion on lettuce. Pour vinaigrette over top. Cover and refrigerate 1 to 2 hours to blend flavors.

2 Sprinkle eggs and croutons over salad. Toss before serving.

Lemon-Garlic Vinaigrette

1/2 cup olive or canola oil

1/4 cup red wine vinegar

2 tablespoons lemon juice

1 teaspoon salt

1/4 teaspoon pepper

1 clove garlic, finely chopped

Shake all ingredients in tightly covered container.

1 SERVING: Calories 165

Fiber 1g	Sodium 340mg
Fat 14g (Saturated 2g)	Protein 3g
Cholesterol 45mg	Carbohydrate 9g

Food Exchanges: 2 Vegetable; 3 Fat

Layered Gazpacho Salad

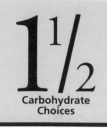

1½
Carbohydrate
Choices

PREP: **5 min**

CHILL: **25 min**

note from **DR. B**

Corn is higher in calories than most other veggies such as broccoli, beans or carrots. As do potatoes and peas, corn has more starch than its more watery relatives, so it belongs in the starch group of the Food Pyramid, not the vegetable group.

"To reduce fat, I use baked tortilla chips for dipping in this great salad and plain yogurt or light sour cream to top it off."
—KATE D.

Corn and Black Bean Salad

6 servings

1 can (15 ounces) black beans, rinsed and drained

1 can (about 8 ounces) whole kernel corn, drained

1 can (4 ounces) chopped green chilies, drained

1/2 cup medium salsa

1/4 cup chopped onion

2 tablespoons chopped fresh cilantro

1 Mix all ingredients in medium bowl.

2 Cover and refrigerate 25 minutes.

---

1 SERVING: Calories 135

Fiber 6g	Sodium 520mg
Fat 1g (Saturated 0g)	Protein 8g
Cholesterol 0mg	Carbohydrate 29g

Food Exchanges: 1 1/2 Starch; 1/2 Very Lean Meat

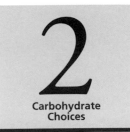

PREP: **15 min**

CHILL: **1 hr**

Garden Couscous Salad

5 servings

2 cups cooked couscous

1 cup sliced zucchini

1 cup garbanzo beans, rinsed and drained

1/4 cup chopped red bell pepper

2 medium green onions, sliced (2 tablespoons)

Yogurt Curry Dressing (below)

Lettuce leaves

1 Mix all ingredients except Yogurt Curry Dressing and lettuce in large bowl.

2 Make Yogurt Curry Dressing; stir into couscous mixture. Cover and refrigerate at least 1 hour to blend flavors but no longer than 6 hours.

3 Serve salad on lettuce.

Yogurt Curry Dressing

1/2 cup plain yogurt

2 tablespoons olive or canola oil

1/2 teaspoon salt

1/4 teaspoon curry powder

Mix all ingredients.

note from **DR. B**
This salad is high in vitamin C from the bell pepper and zucchini. Eating this salad with a food high in iron, such as meat (especially beef), will ensure that the iron from the meat is more easily absorbed into your body.

1 SERVING: Calories 195

Fiber 4g	Sodium 300mg
Fat 7g (Saturated 1g)	Protein 8g
Cholesterol 0mg	Carbohydrate 29g

Food Exchanges: 2 Starch; 1 Fat

Key Lime Fruit Salad

8 servings

1 container (6 ounces) Key lime pie–flavored artificially sweetened low-fat yogurt

2 tablespoons orange juice

2 cups fresh pineapple chunks

1 cup strawberry halves

2 cups green grapes

1 cup blueberries

2 cups cubed cantaloupe

1/4 cup flaked or shredded coconut, toasted*

1 Mix yogurt and orange juice.

2 Layer fruit in order listed in 2 1/2-quart clear glass bowl. Pour yogurt mixture over fruit. Sprinkle with coconut. Serve immediately.

*To toast coconut, heat in ungreased heavy skillet over medium-low heat 6 to 14 minutes, stirring frequently until browning begins, then stirring constantly until golden brown.

1 SERVING: Calories 120

Fiber 3g   Sodium 25mg

Fat 2g   Protein 2g
(Saturated 1g)
                  Carbohydrate
Cholesterol   26g
0mg

Food Exchanges: 2 Fruit

Key Lime Fruit Salad

1 1/2

Carbohydrate Choices

"This portable potato salad is great for a hot summer day. Just keep it well chilled and it's a good traveler to the beach or to a potluck." —BETTY H.

PREP: **15 min**

MICROWAVE: **12 min**

Betty's **success tip**

One way to eat more vegetables is to try new recipes and combinations of vegetables that make them fun. Microwaving vegetables in a small amount of water takes just a few minutes and preserves the vitamins.

Italian New Potato Salad

6 servings

3/4 pound green beans

10 to 12 new potatoes (1 1/2 pounds), cut into fourths

1/4 cup water

1/2 cup Italian dressing or balsamic vinaigrette

1/4 cup chopped red onion

1 can (2 1/4 ounces) sliced ripe olives, drained

1 Cut beans in half if desired. Place beans, potatoes and water in 2-quart microwavable casserole. Cover and microwave on High 10 to 12 minutes, rotating dish 1/2 turn every 4 minutes, just until potatoes are tender; drain.

2 Place beans and potatoes in large glass or plastic bowl. Pour dressing over vegetables; toss. Add onion and olives; toss.

1 SERVING: Calories 180

Fiber 3g	Sodium 280mg
Fat 10g (Saturated 1g)	Protein 3g
Cholesterol 5mg	Carbohydrate 23g

Food Exchanges: 1 Starch; 1 Vegetable; 1 1/2 Fat

1/2
Carbohydrate Choices

Lime-Mint Melon Salad

PREP: 20 min
CHILL: 2 hr

6 servings

1 1/2 cups 1/2-inch cubes honeydew melon (1/2 medium)

1 1/2 cups 1/2-inch cubes cantaloupe (1/2 medium)

1 teaspoon grated lime peel

3 tablespoons lime juice

2 tablespoons chopped fresh or 1 tablespoon dried mint leaves

1 teaspoon honey

1/4 teaspoon salt

1 Toss all ingredients in medium glass or plastic bowl.

2 Cover and refrigerate about 2 hours or until chilled.

Betty's **success tip**

Herbs add a flavor hit to any food they are paired with. Try a bit of fresh rosemary in mashed potatoes, sprinkle fresh oregano over steamed broccoli and chop basil to toss with pasta.

1 SERVING: Calories 40

Fiber 1g	Sodium 110mg
Fat 0g (Saturated 0g)	Protein 1g
Cholesterol 0mg	Carbohydrate 9g

Food Exchanges: 1/2 Fruit

Chapter 8 Don't Forget Desserts

Great news! You don't have to totally give up desserts, even if you have diabetes. The key is moderation and timing. Try one of these great desserts as a snack or a treat after a light, low carbohydrate meal—the choice is yours.

PREP:	**10 min**
BAKE:	**8 to 10 min per sheet**
COOL:	**30 min**

Betty's **success tip**

Citrus fruits add a lot of flavor to foods; orange juice and peel give these easy cookies great flavor. And because these cookies are low-carb, having 2 of them for your snack may fit easily into your eating plan.

"When I bake cookies, I make 1 pan of half-sized cookies and 1 pan of regular cookies for my family. That way, if I feel like eating 2 cookies, I can choose the smaller ones and it still equals just 1 regular cookie." —LYNN H.

Orange Butter Cookies

About 3 1/2 dozen cookies

2/3 cup butter or margarine, softened

3/4 cup sugar

1 egg or 1/4 cup fat-free cholesterol-free egg product

Grated peel of 1 large orange (about 2 tablespoons)

1/2 cup orange juice

2 cups all-purpose flour

1/2 teaspoon baking powder

1/2 teaspoon baking soda

1/2 teaspoon salt

Orange Butter Frosting (below)

1 Heat oven to 350°. Mix butter, sugar and egg in large bowl with spoon until creamy and well blended. Stir in orange peel and orange juice. Stir in remaining ingredients except Orange Butter Frosting.

2 Drop dough by tablespoonfuls about 2 inches apart onto ungreased cookie sheet.

3 Bake 8 to 10 minutes or until light brown around edges. Cool 1 to 2 minutes; remove from cookie sheet to wire rack. Cool completely, about 30 minutes. Frost with Orange Butter Frosting.

Orange Butter Frosting

1 1/2 cups powdered sugar

2 tablespoons butter or margarine, softened

Grated peel of 1 large orange (about 2 tablespoons)

1 1/2 tablespoons orange juice

Mix all ingredients.

1 COOKIE: Calories 90

Fiber 0g	Sodium 75mg
Fat 4g (Saturated 2g)	Protein 1g
	Carbohydrate 13g
Cholesterol 15mg	

Food Exchanges:
1 Carbohydrate; 1 Fat

"I've been trying new recipes since I've been diabetic. This recipe is another winner with a twist to the ordinary, and I was pleasantly surprised to see that 1 cookie is only 1 Carbohydrate Choice. It's fun when I feel that I can eat 'normally.'"

—MICHELLE M.

1
Carbohydrate
Choices

PREP: **15 min**
BAKE: **10 to 12 min per sheet**
COOL: **30 min**

White Chocolate Chunk–Cranberry Cookies

About 5 1/2 dozen cookies

2/3 cup packed brown sugar

1/2 cup granulated sugar

2/3 cup shortening

1/2 cup butter or margarine, softened

1 teaspoon finely shredded orange peel

1 teaspoon vanilla

1 egg or 1/4 cup fat-free cholesterol-free egg product

2 1/4 cups all-purpose flour

1 teaspoon baking soda

1/4 teaspoon salt

2/3 cup dried cranberries

1 package (6 ounces) white baking bars (white chocolate), cut into 1/4- to 1/2-inch chunks

White Chocolate Glaze (below)

1 Heat oven to 350°. Beat sugars, shortening, butter, orange peel, vanilla and egg in large bowl with electric mixer on medium speed until light and fluffy, or mix with spoon. Stir in flour, baking soda and salt. Stir in cranberries and white baking bar chunks.

2 Drop dough by rounded teaspoonfuls about 2 inches apart onto ungreased cookie sheet.

3 Bake 10 to 12 minutes or until light brown. Cool 1 to 2 minutes; remove from cookie sheet to wire rack. Cool completely, about 30 minutes. Drizzle with White Chocolate Glaze.

note from **DR. B**

In desserts, carbohydrate can be contributed by non-fruit, non-starch ingredients like sugar, honey or other sweeteners. The exchange system now lists these as carbohydrate exchanges.

White Chocolate Glaze

1 package (6 ounces) white baking bars (white chocolate), chopped

2 teaspoons shortening

Place ingredients in 2-cup microwavable measuring cup or deep microwavable bowl. Microwave uncovered on High 45 seconds; stir. If baking bars are not melted, microwave 10 to 20 seconds at a time, stirring after each time, until melted.

1 COOKIE: Calories 90

Fiber 0g	Sodium 45mg
Fat 5g (Saturated 2g)	Protein 1g
	Carbohydrate 11g
Cholesterol 10mg	

Food Exchanges:
1 Carbohydrate; 1 Fat

PREP: **15 min**

CHILL: **2 hr**

BAKE: **8 to 10 min
per sheet**

COOL: **30 min**

*"Striving to keep my diabetes in tight control takes planning and effort.
These Double-Ginger Cookies are a sweet reward for all that effort!
While baking, they make the kitchen smell divine."*

—KATE D.

Double-Ginger Cookies

About 5 dozen cookies

3/4 cup sugar

1/4 cup butter or margarine,
softened

1 egg or 1/4 cup fat-free
cholesterol-free egg product

1/4 cup molasses

1 3/4 cups all-purpose flour

1 teaspoon baking soda

1/2 teaspoon ground
cinnamon

1/2 teaspoon ground ginger

1/4 teaspoon ground cloves

1/4 teaspoon salt

1/4 cup sugar

1/4 cup orange marmalade

2 tablespoons finely chopped
crystallized ginger

1 Beat 3/4 cup sugar, the butter, egg and molasses in medium
bowl with electric mixer on medium speed, or mix with spoon.
Stir in flour, baking soda, cinnamon, ground ginger, cloves
and salt. Cover and refrigerate at least 2 hours until firm.

2 Heat oven to 350°. Lightly spray cookie sheet with cooking spray. Shape dough into 3/4-inch balls; roll in 1/4 cup
sugar. Place about 2 inches apart on cookie sheet. Make
indentation in center of each ball, using finger. Fill each
indentation with slightly less than 1/4 teaspoon of the
marmalade. Sprinkle with crystallized ginger.

3 Bake 8 to 10 minutes or until set. Immediately remove
from cookie sheet to wire rack. Cool completely, about
30 minutes.

1 COOKIE: Calories 45

Fiber 0g   Sodium 35mg

Fat 1g   Protein 1g
(Saturated 1g)
              Carbohydrate
Cholesterol   8g
5mg

Food Exchanges:
1/2 Carbohydrate

Double-Ginger Cookies, Orange Butter Cookies (page 218) and White Chocolate Chunk–Cranberry Cookies (page 219)

PREP:	**15 min**
BAKE:	**35 min**
COOL:	**30 min**
CHILL:	**3 hr**

Betty's **success tip**

Graham cracker crumbs are used in this bar instead of high-calorie traditional cookie crumbs. Cutting calories and fat in little ways does add up; in fact, even a couple hundred fewer calories per day adds up to weight loss over time.

"I love dessert, and am so glad I do not have to give it up totally!"

—Tim H.

Key Lime Bars

36 bars

1 1/2 cups graham cracker crumbs (20 squares)

1/3 cup butter or margarine, melted

3 tablespoons sugar

1 package (8 ounces) cream cheese, softened

1 can (14 ounces) sweetened condensed milk

1/4 cup Key lime juice or regular lime juice

1 tablespoon grated lime peel

Additional lime peel, if desired

1 Heat oven to 350°. Grease bottom and sides of square pan, 9 × 9 × 2 inches, with shortening. Mix cracker crumbs, butter and sugar thoroughly with fork. Press evenly in pan. Refrigerate while preparing cream cheese mixture.

2 Beat cream cheese in small bowl with electric mixer on medium speed until light and fluffy. Gradually beat in milk until smooth. Beat in lime juice and lime peel. Spread over layer in pan.

3 Bake about 35 minutes or until center is set. Cool 30 minutes. Cover loosely and refrigerate at least 3 hours until chilled. For bars, cut into 6 rows by 6 rows. Garnish with additional lime peel. Store covered in refrigerator.

1 BAR: Calories 110

Fiber 0g	Sodium 70mg
Fat 6g (Saturated 3g)	Protein 2g
	Carbohydrate 12g
Cholesterol 15mg	

Food Exchanges: 1/2 Starch; 1/2 Fruit; 1 Fat

"Yes! Two of my favorites together—chocolate and oatmeal. That was the one thing about having diabetes that was hard at first—I thought I couldn't eat anything sweet. Now I've found that as long as I stick to my eating plan with the certain number of choices, I can still have a little chocolate and sugar now and then."

—BILL A.

1
Carbohydrate
Choices

PREP: **15 min**
BAKE: **50 min**
COOL: **2 hr 5 min**

Oatmeal Brownies

48 brownies

2 1/2 cups old-fashioned or quick-cooking oats

3/4 cup all-purpose flour

3/4 cup packed brown sugar

1/2 teaspoon baking soda

3/4 cup butter or margarine, melted

1 package (1 pound 6.5 ounces) supreme brownie mix with pouch of chocolate flavor syrup

1/3 cup water

1/3 cup canola or vegetable oil

2 or 3 eggs

1/2 cup chopped nuts

1 Heat oven to 350°. Grease bottom only of rectangular pan, 13 × 9 × 2 inches, with shortening, or spray with cooking spray.

2 Mix oats, flour, brown sugar and baking soda in medium bowl; stir in butter. Reserve 1 cup of the oat mixture. Press remaining oat mixture in pan. Bake 10 minutes; cool 5 minutes.

3 Stir brownie mix, chocolate syrup, water, oil and 2 eggs for fudgelike brownies (or 3 eggs for cakelike brownies) in medium bowl, using spoon, until well blended. Stir in nuts. Spread over baked layer; sprinkle with reserved oat mixture.

4 Bake 35 to 40 minutes or until toothpick inserted 2 inches from side of pan comes out clean or almost clean. Cool completely, about 2 hours. For brownies, cut into 8 rows by 6 rows. Store tightly covered.

note from **DR. B**
Use old-fashioned rolled oats often in your baking. Not only do they add flavor and texture to baked goods, they are also 100 percent whole grain. A recent study discovered that women who ate more whole-grain foods had lower rates of type 2 diabetes.

1 BROWNIE: Calories 135

Fiber 1g   Sodium 80mg

Fat 6g   Protein 2g
(Saturated 3g) Carbohydrate
Cholesterol   19g
15mg

Food Exchanges: 1 Starch;
1 Fat

PREP: **15 min**

BAKE: **8 to 10 min**

CHILL: **2 hr 5 min**

Blueberry-Lemon Tart

12 servings

35 reduced-fat vanilla wafer cookies, crushed (1 1/2 cups)

1 egg white, beaten

1 tablespoon butter or margarine, melted

1 1/4 cups fat-free (skim) milk

1 package (4-serving size) lemon instant pudding and pie filling mix

1 1/2 teaspoons grated lemon peel

1 cup frozen (thawed) fat-free whipped topping

Blueberry Topping (below)

1 Heat oven to 400°. Lightly spray tart pan with removable bottom, 9 × 1 inch, with cooking spray. Mix crushed cookies, egg white and butter until crumbly. Press in bottom and up side of pan. Bake 8 to 10 minutes or until light golden brown; cool.

2 Beat milk, pudding mix and lemon peel in medium bowl with electric mixer on low speed about 2 minutes or until smooth. Refrigerate 5 minutes.

3 Fold whipped topping into pudding mixture. Spread over crust. Cover and refrigerate at least 2 hours until chilled. Serve with Blueberry Topping. Store covered in refrigerator.

Blueberry Topping

2 tablespoons sugar

1 teaspoon cornstarch

3 tablespoons water

1 1/2 cups fresh or frozen blueberries

1 tablespoon lemon juice

Mix sugar, cornstarch and water in 1-quart saucepan. Stir in 1/2 cup of the blueberries. Heat to boiling; reduce heat to medium-low. Cook about 5 minutes or until slightly thickened. Stir in lemon juice; remove from heat. Cool 10 minutes. Stir in remaining 1 cup blueberries. Cover and refrigerate at least 1 hour until chilled.

1 SERVING: Calories 115

Fiber 1g	Sodium 190mg
Fat 2g (Saturated 1g)	Protein 2g
Cholesterol 0mg	Carbohydrate 23g

Food Exchanges: 1/2 Carbohydrate

Blueberry-Lemon Tart

PREP: **10 min**

BAKE: **45 min**

COOL: **30 min**

"My mother used to make custard when we were growing up, and I loved it! Now I make this version as a nourishing dessert for my family. At 1 1/2 Choices, you can't beat it."
—BETTY H.

Baked Custard with Fresh Raspberry Sauce

6 servings

3 eggs, slightly beaten

1/3 cup sugar

1 teaspoon vanilla

Dash of salt

2 1/2 cups very warm milk

Ground nutmeg

Fresh Raspberry Sauce (below)

1 Heat oven to 350°. Mix eggs, sugar, vanilla and salt in medium bowl. Gradually stir in milk. Pour into six 6-ounce custard cups. Sprinkle with nutmeg.

2 Place cups in rectangular pan, 13 × 9 × 2 inches, on oven rack. Pour very hot water into pan to within 1/2 inch of tops of cups.

3 Bake about 45 minutes or until knife inserted halfway between center and edge comes out clean. Remove cups from water. Cool about 30 minutes. Unmold and serve warm with Fresh Raspberry Sauce. Store covered in refrigerator.

Fresh Raspberry Sauce

1 cup fresh or frozen (thawed and drained) raspberries

1 tablespoon water

1 tablespoon sugar

Place all ingredients in food processor. Cover and process until smooth. Press through sieve to remove seeds if desired.

1 SERVING: Calories 155

Fiber 1g	Sodium 80mg
Fat 5g (Saturated 2g)	Protein 7g
	Carbohydrate 21g
Cholesterol 115mg	

Food Exchanges: 1 Skim Milk; 1/2 Fruit; 1 Fat

Healthy Holidays

During the holidays, it may be tempting to go off your meal plan. At a special party or family dinner, you might have an extra helping or more dessert than usual. That's fine! Just get back on your plan the next day.

If you or a member of your family has diabetes, you don't have to completely cross off desserts or holiday goodies. The key is to find something delicious that fits into your (or their) food plan. Whether you're cooking a traditional holiday dinner, bringing a dish to a festive potluck or enjoying yourself at a holiday get-together:

- *Keep up your daily walk* or other exercise to help keep blood glucose down.

- *Stay well rested*, and take care of yourself. You'll be more in control and less tempted to overindulge if you practice healthy habits.

- *Stick to your food plan by planning ahead.* Give up a dinner roll or a helping of potatoes if you really want a wedge of pumpkin pie for dessert.

- *Use lower-fat recipes.* Bake pumpkin (or other) pie without the crust in individual custard cups; lower-fat quick breads, cookies, bars and desserts can be just as tasty as their high-fat counterparts.

- *Eat fewer high-fat, high-calorie treats.* Don't exclude treats altogether, but eat less of them less often.

- *Keep portions small.* If you really love cheesecake, have a small wedge to satisfy your sweet tooth and prevent overindulging on other desserts later.

- *Choose a fun activity*—like a tree-trimming party or an ice-skating party—to take the place of holiday events like cookie exchanges that are centered around food.

- *Drink seltzer water*—but jazz it up! If everyone else is sipping eggnog or another holiday drink, try mixing seltzer with low-calorie cranberry juice for a festive alternative.

- *Bring a dish* that works in your food plan when you're toting something to a potluck dinner. If you like it, chances are everyone else will enjoy it, too.

Snacks and Desserts

Looking for holiday inspiration? These recipes offer you a host of festive—and most of all, delicious—appetizers and desserts worthy of any holiday get-together:

- **Chipotle Black Bean Dip with Lime Tortilla Chips, page 55**

- **Gingered Caramel Dip with Fresh Fruit, page 54**

- **Creamy Vanilla-Caramel Cheesecake, page 232**

- **Baked Custard with Fresh Raspberry Sauce, page 226**

- **Fruit- and Nut-Topped Pound Cake, page 228**

- **Chocolate Dippers, page 236**

"I love eating desserts that contain fruit. That way, I am more likely to get my five servings of fruit and vegetables per day."
—LORI S.

PREP: **10 min**
BROIL: **5 min**

Betty's **success tip**

This fruit and cake dessert can be drizzled with fat-free caramel or another ice-cream topping instead of the chocolate syrup. You can toast the pound cake up to a day ahead and assemble the cake slices and fruit up to 4 hours ahead. Cover and refrigerate until serving.

Fruit- and Nut-Topped Pound Cake

14 servings

1 package (10.75 ounces) frozen pound cake loaf, cut into fourteen 1/2-inch slices

2/3 cup soft cream cheese with strawberries, raspberries or pineapple

1 can (11 ounces) mandarin orange segments, well drained

1 1/2 cups bite-size pieces assorted fresh fruit (kiwifruit, strawberry, raspberry, pear, apple)

1/2 cup reduced-fat chocolate-flavor syrup

1/2 cup sliced almonds or toasted coconut (page 00)

1 Set oven control to broil. Place pound cake slices on rack in broiler pan. Broil with tops 4 to 5 inches from heat 3 to 5 minutes, turning once, until light golden brown.

2 Spread each slice with about 2 teaspoons cream cheese. Cut slices diagonally in half to make 28 pieces. Top with orange segments and desired fresh fruit. Drizzle with syrup; sprinkle with almonds.

1 SERVING: Calories 190

Fiber 2g	Sodium 60mg
Fat 11g (Saturated 4g)	Protein 3g
	Carbohydrate 22g
Cholesterol 35mg	

Food Exchanges: 1 Starch; 1/2 Fruit; 2 Fat

Fruit- and Nut-Topped Pound Cake, Key Lime
(page 222) and Oatmeal Brownies (page 223)

"I find that a light dessert now and then doesn't raise my glucose level as much as pasta, rice and potatoes do, but I did have to use my monitor to figure this out. I keep a list of exactly what foods cause changes in my body." —PAT A.

PREP: **15 min**

FREEZE: **35 min**

note from **DR. B**

Using regular sugar in recipes is okay as long as you count the total carbohydrates. If you want to cut down on sugar in any dessert, reduce it by one-third—it won't make a noticeable difference in the recipe.

Very Berry Frozen Yogurt

12 servings

1 pint (2 cups) strawberries or raspberries

1/3 cup sugar

4 cups vanilla low-fat yogurt

1 Mash strawberries with sugar in large bowl. Stir in yogurt.

2 Pour strawberry mixture into 2-quart ice-cream freezer. Freeze according to manufacturer's directions. Scoop into serving dishes or ice-cream cones.

1 SERVING: Calories 105

Fiber 1g

Fat 1g
(Saturated 1g)

Cholesterol
5mg

Sodium 50mg

Protein 4g

Carbohydrate
23g

Food Exchanges: 1 Fruit;
1/2 Skim Milk

"I love trail mix, and I think of this as a coated trail mix. I like to use cereal in baking because of the extra goodness the cereal provides!" —MICHELE H.

PREP: **10 min**
COOK: **5 min**
STAND: **1 hr**

Vanilla-Cherry Crunch

About 16 servings (1/2 cup each)

3 cups Corn Chex cereal

2 cups tiny fish-shaped pretzels

1 cup dry-roasted peanuts

1 cup miniature marshmallows

1 package (3 ounces) dried cherries (2/3 cup)

12 ounces vanilla-flavored candy coating (almond bark), chopped

1 Toss cereal, pretzels, peanuts, marshmallows and cherries in large bowl.

2 Heat candy coating as directed on package until melted. Pour over cereal mixture; toss gently until coated.

3 Drop mixture by tablespoonfuls onto waxed paper. Let stand about 1 hour or until set. Store loosely covered up to 1 week.

note from **DR. B**
This crunchy dessert makes a tasty snack as well. If snacks are part of your meal plan, planning your snacks is just as important as planning your meals.

1 SERVING: Calories 70

Fiber 1g   Sodium 50mg

Fat 4g   Protein 2g
(Saturated 1g) Carbohydrate
                8g
Cholesterol
0mg

Food Exchanges: 1/2 Starch; 1/2 Fat

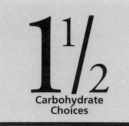

Carbohydrate Choices

PREP: **20 min**

BAKE: **1 hr**

COOL: **45 min**

CHILL: **3 hr**

Betty's **success tip**

Cheesecake doesn't have to be high in fat and calories to be delicious. By replacing full-fat cream cheese and sour cream with their lower-fat counterparts, you can have your cheesecake— and eat it, too!

"Instead of eating dessert with lunch or dinner and going over my Carbohydrate Choices for that meal, I often eat dessert at snack time, using the carbs I'm allowed for snacks."

—KATE D.

Creamy Vanilla-Caramel Cheesecake

16 servings

15 reduced-fat chocolate or vanilla wafer cookies, crushed (1/2 cup)

2 packages (8 ounces each) reduced-fat cream cheese (Neufchâtel), softened

2/3 cup sugar

3 egg whites or 1/2 cup fat-free cholesterol-free egg product

2 teaspoons vanilla

2 cups vanilla low-fat yogurt

2 tablespoons all-purpose flour

1/3 cup fat-free caramel topping

Pecan halves, if desired

1 Heat oven to 300°. Spray springform pan, 9 × 3 inches, with cooking spray. Sprinkle cookie crumbs over bottom of pan.

2 Beat cream cheese in medium bowl with electric mixer on medium speed until smooth. Add sugar, egg whites and vanilla. Beat on medium speed about 2 minutes or until smooth. Add yogurt and flour. Beat on low speed until smooth.

3 Carefully spread batter over cookie crumbs in pan. Bake 1 hour. Turn off oven; cool in oven 30 minutes with door closed. Remove from oven; cool 15 minutes. Cover and refrigerate at least 3 hours.

4 Drizzle caramel topping over cheesecake. Garnish with pecan halves. Store covered in the refrigerator.

1 SERVING: Calories 175

Fiber 0g

Fat 7g
(Saturated 5g)

Cholesterol 25mg

Sodium 180mg

Protein 5g

Carbohydrate 23g

Food Exchanges:
2 Carbohydrate; 1 Fat

Creamy Vanilla-Caramel Cheesecake

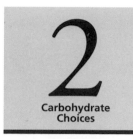

2

Carbohydrate
Choices

PREP: **10 min**
BAKE: **35 min**
COOL: **15 min**

Betty's **success tip**

This cake tastes best when eaten warm. So try wrapping remaining pieces individually and warm in the microwave on High for 20 seconds for a 2-Carbohydrate-Choice snack.

"I no longer think about having dessert with my lunch since I can have only 4 Carbohydrate Choices per meal. If I really want a sweet treat, I save it and have a small piece for my afternoon snack—that way it's so much more enjoyable."

—KATE D.

Chocolate Snack Cake

10 servings

1 1/2 cups all-purpose flour

1 cup sugar

1/4 cup baking cocoa

1 teaspoon baking soda

1/2 teaspoon salt

1/3 cup canola or vegetable oil

1 teaspoon white vinegar

1/2 teaspoon vanilla

1 cup cold water

1 Heat oven to 350°. Grease bottom and side of round pan, 9 × 1 1/2 inches, or square pan, 8 × 8 × 2 inches, with shortening; lightly flour.

2 Mix flour, sugar, cocoa, baking soda and salt in medium bowl. Mix oil, vinegar and vanilla in measuring cup. Vigorously stir oil mixture and water into flour mixture about 1 minute or until well blended. Immediately pour into pan.

3 Bake 30 to 35 minutes or until toothpick inserted in center comes out clean. Cool 15 minutes. Serve warm.

1 SERVING: Calories 215

Fiber 1g

Fat 8g
(Saturated 1g)

Cholesterol
0mg

Sodium
240mg

Protein 2g

Carbohydrate
35g

Food Exchanges:
2 Carbohydrate; 1 1/2 Fat

Sugar News

People with diabetes were once taught that the only way they could enjoy sweet foods was to use sugar substitutes. Times have changed! In 1994, the American Diabetes Association relaxed its ban on sugar because studies show that table sugar doesn't raise blood glucose any more quickly than other carbohydrates such as pasta, rice or potatoes.

Although you don't have to cut out all sugar, paying attention to the amount of sugar you eat and counting carbohydrates (see page 11) is still the key to maintaining blood glucose control. When eating sugar-containing foods:

- *Substitute sweets* for other carbohydrates in your food plan. Don't "add" them.

- *Satisfy your sweet tooth* with a small amount of your favorite treat.

- *Eat smaller portions.* A piece of fudge or candy can fit into your food plan—but that's only if you have a small serving of one to two pieces.

- *Test your blood glucose* after eating foods containing different sugars and sweets; let that determine how much or how often you consume these foods, or if you need to adjust your insulin dose.

- *Share desserts* with others when dining out. Restaurant desserts can be very rich—a bite or two is all you may need to feel like you've truly indulged!

- *Choose an artificially sweetened version* of your regular beverage. Most hot cocoas, colas, iced teas and other drinks come in sugar-free sweetened versions.

- *Select a few favorites* and decide in light of your personal goals how often to eat them, perhaps twice a week or only on special occasions.

Sweet Substitutes

You may still want to use sugar substitutes once in a while. They're "free" foods so you don't have to count them as carbohydrates.

- *Calorie-free sweeteners* such as *aspartame*, *saccharin*, and *sucralose* won't increase your blood glucose level.

- *Sugar alcohols,* such as *xylitol*, *mannitol*, and *sorbitol*, often found in sugar-free candies and gum, do have some calories and may slightly increase blood glucose levels.

- When choosing what recipe to make, it's helpful to know that 1 tablespoon of sugar has 12 grams of carbohydrate.

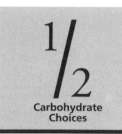

Carbohydrate Choices

PREP: **15 min**
COOK: **5 min**
CHILL: **30 min**

Betty's **success tip**

For Vanilla Dippers, use 6 ounces vanilla-flavored candy coating (almond bark), cut up, for the chocolate chips. To make Double Dippers, dip fruit into melted chocolate chips, then drizzle with melted vanilla-flavored candy coating or sprinkle with crushed candies.

"I was so glad to find this easy, acceptable treat for my two chocolate-loving children with diabetes. It would be fun to make this and take it to a party."

—BETTY H.

Chocolate Dippers

3 to 4 dozen pieces

1 bag (6 ounces) semisweet chocolate chips (1 cup)

1 tablespoon shortening

3 to 4 dozen assorted dippers (dried apricots, strawberries, maraschino cherries, pretzels, small cookies, angel food or pound cake cubes)

Colored sugar or candy decors, if desired

1 Line jelly roll pan, 15 1/2 × 10 1/2 × 1 inch, with waxed paper. Heat chocolate chips and shortening in heavy 1-quart saucepan over low heat, stirring frequently, until smooth; remove from heat.

2 Dip any of the assorted dippers 3/4 of the way into chocolate; sprinkle with sugar. Place on waxed paper in pan.

3 Refrigerate uncovered about 30 minutes or until chocolate is firm.

3 PIECES: Calories 50

Fiber 1g   Sodium 25mg

Fat 2g
(Saturated 1g)   Protein 0g

Cholesterol   Carbohydrate
0mg   7 g

Food Exchanges: 1/2 Fruit; 1/2 Fat

Chocolate Dippers

Menus for 7 Days

To make your life simpler, here is a week's worth of menus. Think of them as ideas for healthy, quick meals and snacks that center around **Carbohydrate Choices**. The suggested foods are lower in fat and calories and high in fiber, and many are based on recipes found in this cookbook. To add variety, mix and match meals and snacks from different days and customize them to meet your individual needs.

Planning meals and snacks based on Carbohydrate Choices doesn't have to be difficult, especially if you begin with the suggestions here. The meals are based on 3 to 4 Choices and snacks are 1 to 2 Choices.

Monday Menu

Breakfast

1 serving **Carrot-Lemon Bread** *(page 41)*

1/2 cup raspberries or blueberries

1 cup fat-free (skim) milk

Carbohydrate Choices 3^1/$_2$ • Calories 330

Snack

1 small banana

Carbohydrate Choices 1 • Calories 225

Lunch

1 serving **Garbanzo Bean Sandwiches** *(page 153)*

Spinach Salad with 2 tablespoons reduced-fat Caesar dressing

1 orange, tangerine or clementine

1 cup fat-free (skim) milk

Carbohydrate Choices 4 • Calories 460

Snack

15 mini pretzel twists (3/4 oz.)

1 cup artificially sweetened light yogurt

1 cup hot herbal tea or coffee

Carbohydrate Choices 2 • Calories 185

Dinner

1 serving **Calypso Shrimp with Black Bean Salsa** *(page 105)*

2/3 cup cooked rice or pasta

1 serving **Lime-Mint Melon Salad** *(page 215)*

1 cup sparkling water

Carbohydrate Choices 4 • Calories 470

Snack

3 graham cracker squares

12 fresh sweet cherries

1 cup hot herb tea

Carbohydrate Choices 2 • Calories 140

DAILY TOTAL • 18^1/$_2$ Carbohydrate Choices

Calories 1600 • Fat 36g • Cholesterol 195mg • Saturated Fat 6g • Protein 85g • Fiber 38g

Tuesday Menu

Breakfast

1 serving **Cinnamon-Raisin Snack Mix** *(page 64)*

1 serving **Watermelon-Kiwi-Banana Smoothie** *(page 66)*

Carbohydrate Choices 4 • Calories 270

Snack

1/2 bagel with 1 tablespoon reduced-fat cream cheese

Carbohydrate Choices 1^1/$_2$ • Calories 175

Lunch

1 serving **Countryside Pasta Toss** *(page 158)*

10 baby-cut carrots with 2 tablespoons **Roasted Vegetable Dip** *(page 56)*

1 cup fat-free (skim) milk

Carbohydrate Choices 4^1/$_2$ • Calories 400

Snack

1 **Orange Butter Cookie** *(page 218)*

1 cup fat-free (skim) milk

Carbohydrate Choices 1^1/$_2$ • Calories 175

Dinner

1 baked pork chop

1 serving **Oven-Fried Potato Wedges** *(page 196)*

1 serving **Broccoli and Tomatoes with Herbs** *(page 199)*

1 small pear

Carbohydrate Choices 3^1/$_2$ • Calories 550

Snack

3 oz. red or green seedless grapes (about 17 grapes)

Carbohydrate Choices 1 • Calories 60

DAILY TOTAL • 16 Carbohydrate Choices

Calories 1500 • Fat 35g • Saturated Fat 16g • Cholesterol 130mg • Protein 100g • Fiber 21g

Wednesday Menu

Breakfast

2 slices whole-wheat toast with 2 tablespoons peanut butter

1 small banana

1 cup tea or coffee

Carbohydrate Choices 4 • Calories 420

Snack

1 cup **Chai Tea** *(page 68)*

1 small muffin, 1 1/2 ounces

Carbohydrate Choices 2 • Calories 200

Lunch

1 serving **Key Lime Fruit Salad** *(page 212)*

1 roast beef (3 ounces) sandwich with 2 slices whole wheat bread and 2 teaspoons mustard

1 cup raw broccoli flowerets and cauliflowerets

1 cup hot tea or coffee

Carbohydrate Choices 4 • Calories 500

Snack

1 **White Chocolate Chunk–Cranberry Cookie** *(page 219)*

1 cup fat-free (skim) milk

Carbohydrate Choices 1^1/$_2$ • Calories 175

Dinner

1 serving **Honey-Mustard Turkey with Snap Peas** *(page 94)*

1 serving **Corn and Black Bean Salad** *(page 210)*

1 serving **Harvest Roasted Vegetables** *(page 198)*

1 cup fat-free (skim) milk

Carbohydrate Choices 4 • Calories 430

Snack

1 cup artificially sweetened fruited light yogurt

Carbohydrate Choices 1 • Calories 80

DAILY TOTAL • 17^1/$_2$ Carbohydrate Choices

Calories 1750 • Fat 43g • Saturated Fat 13g • Cholesterol 215mg • Protein 122g • Fiber 30g

Thursday Menu

Breakfast

1/2 cup high-fiber cereal

1 1/4 cup whole strawberries

1 cup fat-free (skim) milk

Carbohydrate Choices 3 • **Calories 210**

Snack

1 serving **Oatmeal Brownies** *(page 223)*

1 cup hot herbal tea

Carbohydrate Choices 1 • **Calories 135**

Lunch

1 serving **Beef-Barley Stew** *(page 176)*

1 serving **Hearty Multigrain Biscuits** *(page 71)*

1 medium apple

Carbohydrate Choices 4 • **Calories 500**

Snack

3/4 oz. reduced-fat whole-wheat crackers (about 6)

1/4 cup cottage cheese

2 tablespoons sunflower nuts

Carbohydrate Choices 1 • **Calories 230**

Dinner

1 serving **Potato-Tomato-Tofu Dinner** *(page 166)*

1 small whole-wheat dinner roll

1 serving **Mediterranean Vegetable Salad** *(page 207)*

1 cup fat-free (skim) milk

Carbohydrate Choices 4 • **Calories 630**

Snack

3 cups popped light popcorn

1 cup (fat-free) sugar free hot cocoa

Carbohydrate Choices 1$^1/_2$ • **Calories 150**

DAILY TOTAL • 15$^1/_2$ Carbohydrate Choices

Calories 1725 • Fat 63g • Saturated Fat 22g • Cholesterol 165mg •
Protein 93g • Fiber 42g

Friday Menu

Breakfast

1 serving **Country Ham and Asparagus Bake** *(page 32)*

1/2 cup calcium-fortified orange juice

1 cup latte

Carbohydrate Choices 4 • **Calories 410**

Snack

12 to 15 green or red seedless grapes

Carbohydrate Choices 1 • **Calories 80**

Lunch

1 serving **Zesty Autumn Pork Stew** *(page 178)*

1 **Parmesan-Herb Breadstick** *(page 69)*

1 kiwifruit

1 cup fat-free (skim) milk

Carbohydrate Choices 4 • **Calories 490**

Snack

1 whole-grain granola bar (1 ounce)

1 cup hot herbal tea

Carbohydrate Choices 1 • **Calories 100**

Dinner

1 serving **Halibut with Lime and Cilantro** *(page 96)*

1 serving **Bulgur Pilaf** *(page 137)*

Mixed-greens salad with 2 tablespoons Caesar dressing

1 serving **Very Berry Frozen Yogurt** *(page 230)*

Carbohydrate Choices 3 • **Calories 500**

Snack

1 cup fat-free (skim) milk

3 **Chocolate Dippers** *(page 236)*

Carbohydrate Choices 2 • **Calories 190**

DAILY TOTAL • 16 Carbohydrate Choices

Calories 1700 • Fat 55g • Saturated Fat 24g • Cholesterol 468mg •
Protein 141g • Fiber 25g

Saturday Menu

Breakfast

1 serving **Oatmeal Pancakes with Maple-Cranberry Syrup** *(page 46)*

1 serving reduced-fat beef or pork sausage

1 cup fat-free (skim) milk

Carbohydrate Choices 4 • **Calories 500**

Snack

1 cup melon cubes

Carbohydrate Choices 1 • **Calories 55**

Lunch

1 serving **Veggies and Cheese Mini-Pizzas** *(page 58)*

1 serving **Triple-Fruit Yogurt Smoothie** *(page 67)*

1 medium apple

Carbohydrate Choices 3$^1/_2$ • **Calories 370**

Snack

1 serving **Hiker's Trail Mix** *(page 62)*

1 cup fat free, aspartame sweetened hot cocoa

Carbohydrate Choices 2 • **Calories 230**

Dinner

1 serving **Fajita Salad** *(page 120)*

1 **Cheddar and Green Onion Biscuit** *(page 74)*

1 cup steamed green beans

1 serving **Key Lime Bars** *(page 222)*

1 cup fat-free (skim) milk

Carbohydrate Choices 4 • **Calories 635**

Snack

1 serving **Gingered Caramel Dip with Fresh Fruit** *(page 54)*

1 cup hot tea or coffee or water

Carbohydrate Choices 1 • **Calories 110**

DAILY TOTAL • 15$^1/_2$ Carbohydrate Choices

Calories 1900 • **Fat 60g** • **Saturated Fat 20g** • **Cholesterol 180mg** •
Protein 87g • **Fiber 23g**

Sunday Menu

Breakfast

1 **Double-Berry Muffin** *(page 40)*

1 pear

1 cup fat-free (skim) milk

Carbohydrate Choices 4$^1/_2$ • **Calories 330**

Snack

1/2 cup unsweetened applesauce

Carbohydrate Choices 1 • **Calories 95**

Lunch

1 serving **Crunchy Chicken Chunks with Thai Peanut Sauce** *(page 60)*

1 serving **Garden Couscous Salad** *(page 211)*

1 serving **Tomato-Basil Crostini** *(page 72)*

1 cup fat-free (skim) milk

Carbohydrate Choices 4 • **Calories 510**

Snack

1 serving **Chipotle Black Bean Dip with Lime Tortilla Chips** *(page 55)*

Carbohydrate Choices 1 • **Calories 175**

Dinner

1 serving **Vegetables and Cheese Frittata** *(page 31)*

1 serving **Savory Sweet Potato Pan Bread** *(page 70)*

1/3 cup mixed fresh fruit

1 cup steamed green beans

Carbohydrate Choices 3$^1/_2$ • **Calories 470**

Snack

1 serving **Baked Custard with Fresh Raspberry Sauce** *(page 226)*

1 cup hot herbal tea

Carbohydrate Choices 1$^1/_2$ • **Calories 155**

DAILY TOTAL • 15$^1/_2$ Carbohydrate Choices

Calories 1735 • **Fat 59g** • **Saturated Fat 19g** • **Cholesterol 544mg** •
Protein 85g • **Fiber 21g**

Glossary of Diabetes Terms

Listed below are definitions of the nutrition and medical terms used in this cookbook.

Antioxidants: Substances that inhibit oxidation in plant and animal cells. May be important in preventing heart and blood vessel disease.

Blood Glucose: The main sugar that the body makes from the foods we eat, mostly from carbohydrate. Without insulin, the cells cannot use glucose for energy.

Calcium: Found in dairy foods, this mineral is important for maintaining strong bones and teeth and proper nerve and muscle function.

Carbohydrate: Providing quick energy, carbohydrates are the body's main fuel source.

Carbohydrate Counting: A system of "counting" carbohydrate foods, the foods that primarily cause blood glucose levels to go up.

Cholesterol: A fatlike substance found in animal foods that is important for cell structures, hormones and nerve coverings. LDL (low-density lipoprotein), or "bad" cholesterol, increases the risk of heart disease. HDL (high-density lipoprotein), or "good" cholesterol, protects against heart disease.

Chromium: A trace mineral that works with insulin to help the body use glucose, it is found in meats, eggs, whole grains and cheese.

Coronary Heart Disease (CHD): A buildup of fatty, cholesterol-filled deposits in the arteries of the heart that block the normal flow of blood and can ultimately cause a heart attack.

Diabetes: A disease that occurs when the body is not able to use glucose (a form of sugar produced from the digestion of carbohydrate foods) for energy, either at all, or properly.

Diabetes Care Team: Doctor, nurse, registered dietitian, health psychologist, pharmacist and others that may be involved in the care and management of diabetes.

Diabetes Food Guide Pyramid: A nutrition education guide developed to help people with diabetes learn how to eat a healthy balance of a variety of foods.

Dietitian: A registered dietitian (RD) is recognized by the medical community as the primary provider of nutrition education and counseling.

Fat: A necessary nutrient, fat helps build new cells, shuttles vitamins through the body and makes certain hormones that regulate blood pressure.

Fiber: The type of carbohydrate in a food that is not broken down before passing through the body to be eliminated.

Food Exchanges: Developed by the American Dietetic Association and the American Diabetes Association, Food Exchanges categorize foods based on their nutritional content. Sometimes called Diet Exchanges.

Free Foods: Food or drink that has less than 20 calories or less than 5 grams of carbohydrates per serving.

Gestational Diabetes: A type of diabetes that can occur in the second half of a woman's pregnancy.

Glucose: A simple sugar formed from carbohydrate foods during the digestion process. It goes from the bloodstream to the body's cells, where it is the body's main source of energy.

Glycemic Index: A controversial rating system that predicts how high the blood glucose level will rise after eating specific foods.

Hemoglobin A$_{1c}$: A blood test that measures the average blood glucose over two to three months. This test is closely related to a person's risk for developing diabetes complications.

Herbs: Plants or parts of plants that impart flavor and may have medicine-like qualities.

High Blood Pressure (Hypertension): Occurs when blood pressure is equal to or greater than 140/90 millimeters of mercury for the general population, or 130/80 for people with diabetes.

Hyperglycemia: A high blood glucose level; it is a sign that diabetes is out of control.

Hypoglycemia: A low blood glucose level; it is a sign that food, exercise and medication are not properly balanced in diabetes. It is often characterized by sweatiness, shakiness and confusion.

Insulin: A hormone made by islet cells in the pancreas that helps the body use glucose for energy.

Insulin-sensitizing agents: Medications that help the body use insulin more efficiently. These medications reduce insulin resistance and help improve blood glucose control in type 2 diabetes.

Insulin-stimulating agents: Medications that stimulate the cells of the pancreas to release more insulin to help lower blood glucose levels in type 2 diabetes.

Iron: A mineral that carries oxygen to cells, iron is vital for life and is found in meats, spinach and fortified cereal.

Meditation: Quiet forms of contemplation and mindfulness used to establish a sense of peace, inner calm and relaxation.

Minerals: Organic compounds, needed in very small amounts, that help the body with many functions.

Monounsaturated Fat: Good fat found in canola oil, olive oil, nuts and avocados.

Nutrients: Substances necessary for life that build, repair and maintain body cells. Protein, carbohydrates, fats, water, vitamins and minerals are nutrients.

Phytochemicals: Many naturally occurring substances found in plant foods that may have disease-fighting properties.

Polyunsaturated Fat: Good fat found in corn oil, soybean oil and sunflower oil.

Protein: This nutrient builds cells and makes hormones and enzymes that help the body function and generates antibodies to fight infection.

Saturated Fat: Solid at room temperature, these fats tend to elevate blood cholesterol levels and come from animal sources: beef, pork, poultry, eggs and dairy foods. Palm and coconut oils, which come from plants, are also saturated fats, even though they are liquids.

Sugar Alcohols: A group of sugars that are often used instead of table sugar in diet foods.

Triglycerides: A type of fat found in the blood. Being overweight and consuming too much fat, alcohol or sugar can increase blood triglycerides.

Type 1 Diabetes: A chronic disease that occurs mostly in children and young adults; the immune system attacks the pancreas which over time stops producing insulin. Daily insulin injections are required.

Type 2 Diabetes: A disease that occurs mostly in adults over the age of 40, although it is now being seen in growing numbers of children and young adults; the pancreas makes insulin but the body does not use it properly. It is the most common form of diabetes and is related to obesity and inactivity.

Unsaturated Fat: Liquid at room temperature, these fats do not tend to elevate blood cholesterol levels. They are from plant sources and include olive oil, sunflower oil, corn oil, nuts and avocados.

Vitamins: A group of vital nutrients, found in small amounts in a variety of foods, that are key to developing cells, controlling body functions and helping release energy from fuel sources.

Whole Grains: The entire edible part of any grain: the bran, endosperm and germ. Experts recommend eating at least three servings of whole grains every day for optimal health.

Yoga: An ancient practice based on deep breathing, stretching and strengthening exercises to balance the mind, body and spirit.

Carbohydrate Choices of Common Foods

A **Carbohydrate Choice** is the amount of a food that has about 15 grams of carbohydrate. (To read more about **Carbohydrate Choices**, see page 7.) Here are some common foods and the number of **Carbohydrate Choices** they contain:

Food	Carbohydrate Choices
Grains / Beans / Starchy Vegetables	
Bagel, 1 large (most bagel shops)	4
Baked beans, 1/2 cup	1 1/2
Beans (pinto, garbanzo, kidney), cooked, 1/2 cup	1
Bread, 1 slice, 1 ounce	1
Cereal, unsweetened, 3/4 cup	1
Dinner roll, 1 ounce	1
English muffin, 2 ounces	2
Hamburger or hot dog bun, 2 ounces	2
Pancakes, 4 inches across, 2 pancakes	1
Pasta (macaroni, noodles, spaghetti), cooked, 1/3 cup	1
Rice, white or brown, cooked, 1/3 cup	1
Potato, baked or boiled, 1 medium	2
Potato, mashed, 1/2 cup	1
Tortilla, 6 inches across, 1 tortilla	1
Waffle, 4 1/2 inches across, 1 waffle	1

Food	Carbohydrate Choices
Fruits / Fruit Juices	
Apple, orange or pear, 1 medium	1
Banana, 1 medium	2
Blueberries, raspberries or strawberries, 1 cup	1
Cherries or grapes, 12 to 15	1
Grapefruit, 1/2 medium	1
Honeydew melon, cantaloupe or watermelon, 1 cup	1
Orange juice, 1/3 to 1/2 cup	1
Prunes, 3	1
Raisins, 2 tablespoons	1
Milk, Yogurt, Milk Substitutes	
Milk, fat-free (skim), 1% or 2%, 1 cup	1
Soy milk, low-fat or nonfat, 1 cup	1
Yogurt, low-fat, artificially sweetened or plain, 3/4 to 1 cup	1
Yogurt, low-fat, sweetened with fruit, 3/4 to 1 cup	2–3

Food	Carbohydrate Choices
Snacks / Sweets	
Brownie or cake, frosted, 2 inches square	2
Chips, potato or tortilla, 10 to 15 chips or 3/4 ounce	1
Chocolate snack-size candy bar, 1 ounce	1
Crackers, graham, 3 squares	1
Crackers, saltines, 6 squares	1
Crackers, snack, 4 or 5 crackers	1
Doughnut, glazed, 3 inches across	2
Frozen yogurt, nonfat or low-fat, 1/2 cup	1 1/2
Gelatin, regular (not sugar-free), 1/2 cup	1
Hard candies, 3 round	1
Ice cream or light ice cream, 1/2 cup	1
Jam or jelly, regular, 1 tablespoon	1
Muffin, 2 ounce	2
Pudding, sugar-free, 1/2 cup	1
Sugar (table), syrup or honey, 1 tablespoon	1

Food	Carbohydrate Choices
Combination Foods	
Burrito, bean, flour tortilla, 7 inches long	3
Burrito, meat, flour tortilla, 7 inches long	2
Chili or casserole, 1 cup	2
Hamburger with bun, regular size	2
Lasagna, 3 × 4 inches piece	2
Macaroni and cheese, 1 cup	2
Pasta or potato salad, 1/2 cup	1
Pizza, thick crust, 1/8 pizza	2
Pizza, thin crust, 1/8 pizza	1
Soup, bean, cream, noodle or vegetable, 1 cup	1
Spaghetti or pasta sauce, canned, 1/2 cup	1
Sub sandwich, 6 inches long	3
Taco, 1	1

Metric Conversion Guide

Volume

U.S. Units	Canadian Metric	Australian Metric
1/4 teaspoon	1 mL	1 ml
1/2 teaspoon	2 mL	2 ml
1 teaspoon	5 mL	5 ml
1 tablespoon	15 mL	20 ml
1/4 cup	50 mL	60 ml
1/3 cup	75 mL	80 ml
1/2 cup	125 mL	125 ml
2/3 cup	150 mL	170 ml
3/4 cup	175 mL	190 ml
1 cup	250 mL	250 ml
1 quart	1 liter	1 liter
1 1/2 quarts	1.5 liters	1.5 liters
2 quarts	2 liters	2 liters
2 1/2 quarts	2.5 liters	2.5 liters
3 quarts	3 liters	3 liters
4 quarts	4 liters	4 liters

Weight

U.S. Units	Canadian Metric	Australian Metric
1 ounce	30 grams	30 grams
2 ounces	55 grams	60 grams
3 ounces	85 grams	90 grams
4 ounces (1/4 pound)	115 grams	125 grams
8 ounces (1/2 pound)	225 grams	225 grams
16 ounces (1 pound)	455 grams	500 grams
1 pound	455 grams	1/2 kilogram

Note: The recipes in this cookbook have not been developed or tested using metric measures. When converting recipes to metric, some variations in quality may be noted.

Measurements

Inches	Centimeters
1	2.5
2	5.0
3	7.5
4	10.0
5	12.5
6	15.0
7	17.5
8	20.5
9	23.0
10	25.5
11	28.0
12	30.5
13	33.0

Temperatures

Fahrenheit	Celsius
32°	0°
212°	100°
250°	120°
275°	140°
300°	150°
325°	160°
350°	180°
375°	190°
400°	200°
425°	220°
450°	230°
475°	240°
500°	260°

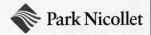

International Diabetes Center
Park Nicollet

A Leader in Diabetes Education and Care

International Diabetes Center at Park Nicollet provides world-class diabetes management, education and research programs to meet the needs of people with diabetes and their families. Located in Minneapolis, Minnesota, the center is internationally recognized for its range of clinical, motivational and educational programs, products and services. Founded in 1967, International Diabetes Center's mission is to ensure that every individual with diabetes or at risk for diabetes receives the best possible care.

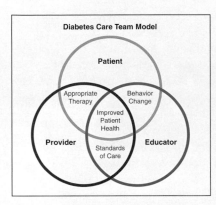

Diabetes Care Team Model

Patient

Appropriate Therapy

Behavior Change

Improved Patient Health

Provider

Educator

Standards of Care

Helping People Live Well with Diabetes

The center's guiding principle is that patient-centered, team care is the key to excellent diabetes management. Its outpatient care programs, educational products and professional training programs reflect this philosophy. From classes that teach basic self-care skills to consulting services that improve clinical care systems, the center provides education and support for adults, children and their families and their primary care providers.

Expertise Based on Research and Innovation

International Diabetes Center has conducted more than 200 clinical trials to date, including the landmark *Diabetes Control and Complications Trial* and groundbreaking work demonstrating the important roles that dietitians and diabetes nurse specialists have in diabetes care. Results of this work and extensive clinical experience are the foundation of its evidence-based approaches to education and care. The center is dedicated to sharing its methods and knowledge with other healthcare organizations to help them achieve the best possible outcomes for patients with diabetes.

Worldwide Training

International Diabetes Center trains health professionals in the most current diabetes care practices, works to improve diabetes screening and detection practices and educates the public about the disease—all on a worldwide basis. International Diabetes Center professionals travel across the country and around the world to consult with, train and coach healthcare providers and administrators as they improve their own practices and patient outcomes. Today, healthcare centers in Mexico, Brazil, Singapore, Japan, Poland and the United States are among the many organizations that have embraced International Diabetes Center's education and care solutions.

Visit Us Online

To learn more about International Diabetes Center, or for comprehensive information about diabetes prevention, care, education and research, visit www.internationaldiabetescenter.com or call 1-888-825-6315.

Patient Services

Annual diabetes assessment and checkup

Classes and educational materials

Coaching and motivational mastery

Counseling

Clinical research Health & Care Stores

Professional Services

Medical education and training

Fellowships and internships

Patient education curriculums

Clinical guidelines and tools

Care systems consulting

Index

Note: *Italicized* page references indicate photographs.

Complete your cookbook library
with these *Betty Crocker* titles

Betty Crocker's A Passion for Pasta

Betty Crocker's Best Bread Machine Cookbook

Betty Crocker's Best Chicken Cookbook

Betty Crocker's Best Christmas Cookbook

Betty Crocker's Best of Baking

Betty Crocker's Best of Healthy and Hearty Cooking

Betty Crocker's Best-Loved Recipes

Betty Crocker's Bisquick® Cookbook

Betty Crocker's Bread Machine Cookbook

Betty Crocker's Cook It Quick

Betty Crocker's Cookbook, 9th Edition - *The* **BIG RED** *Cookbook*®

Betty Crocker's Cookbook, Bridal Edition

Betty Crocker's Cookie Book

Betty Crocker's Cooking for Two

Betty Crocker's Cooky Book, Facsimile Edition

Betty Crocker's Cooking Basics

Betty Crocker's Easy Slow Cooker Dinners

Betty Crocker's Eat and Lose Weight

Betty Crocker's Entertaining Basics

Betty Crocker's Flavors of Home

Betty Crocker's Great Grilling

Betty Crocker's Healthy New Choices

Betty Crocker's Indian Home Cooking

Betty Crocker's Italian Cooking

Betty Crocker's Kids Cook!

Betty Crocker's Kitchen Library

Betty Crocker's Living with Cancer

Betty Crocker's Low-Fat Low-Cholesterol Cooking Today

Betty Crocker's New Cake Decorating

Betty Crocker's New Chinese Cookbook

Betty Crocker's Picture Cook Book, Facsimile Edition

Betty Crocker's Quick & Easy Cookbook

Betty Crocker's Slow Cooker Cookbook

Betty Crocker's Southwest Cooking

Betty Crocker's Ultimate Cake Mix Cookbook

Betty Crocker's Vegetarian Cooking